19 95/80K

D1071121

General and Industrial
MANAGEMENT

OTHER IEEE PRESS BOOKS

General and Industrial MANAGEMENT

Henri Fayol

Revised by

Irwin Gray

Professor of Management
New York Institute of Technology

IEEE
PRESS

Published under the sponsorship of the IEEE Engineering Management Society.

The Institute of Electrical and Electronics Engineers, Inc., New York

A revised and updated edition of *General and Industrial Management* by Henri Fayol, copyright 1949 by Pitman Publishing Corporation. Revised edition, published with permission of Pitman Learning, Inc.

IEEE Order Number: PC01727

Library of Congress Cataloging in Publication Data

Fayol, Henri, 1841–1925.
    General and industrial managment.

    Translation of: Administration industrielle et générale.
    "Published under the sponsorship of the IEEE Engineering Management Society."
    Includes index.
    1. Industrial management. 2. Management. I. Gray, Irwin. II. Title.
HD31.F313   1984   658   84-10747
ISBN 0-87942-178-9

Contents

7 Controlling 57

8 General Principles of Managing the Body Corporate 61

9 The Various Abilities Needed by a Firm's Personnel 83

Foreword: Two Viewpoints

FROM AN EXECUTIVE IN INDUSTRY

As one whose respect for Henri Fayol borders on veneration, I hardly consider myself qualified to write a foreword to a work of this magnitude. Rather, let us consider this section a reflection on this classic work by a modern day practicing manager.

First, we must wonder why "desecrate" such a classic by a modern "revision." I would say for the same reason one would seek a modern translation of the Bible—to free the reader from the difficulties of sifting through language and thought that are limited to the time and place of composition, and thus allow him to directly contact the applicable message. The original work certainly continues to exist for those with a "pure" interest, but for most of us this book is the preferable route to finding Fayol's message, and there is indeed one here.

In his biography, Fayol is referred to as a philosopher of administration. Fittingly, this revision yields a philosophical book, one which is humanistic. It is a thoughtful look back over Fayol's long and successful career in business management.

Writing early in this century, Fayol knew that management was not a science—just as it is not today. There are no known formulas for success. Management consists of dealing with people, with all the vagaries inherent in such activity, and Fayol obviously possessed a vast knowledge of what makes human beings tick—especially in an organizational environment. That is why his conclusions are both original and timeless.

Fayol was trying to save us the pain of management failure. He observed that "experiences....are expensive teachers." Here is a man who observed so many mistakes in management—probably his own initially and later on in others—that he felt compelled to codify what he had learned. Although a "natural" manager, he believed the management process could be taught. But read carefully! Fayol goes beyond the mere mechanics of a fixed methodology. He emphasized morals and tact even as his prescriptions were so tactfully stated that they could easily go over our heads.

It is easy to see the timelessness of his thoughts. Just observe the breadth of his insights. Here is a nineteenth century manager who has scooped all of us in emphasizing such aspects of management as physical fitness and health, incentive programs, and the problems of an over-aggressive staff. What then is new in the twentieth century? Not only are we reinventing Fayol's wheel, but we discover that Fayol went beyond us to develop ideas we do not even find among today's new management concepts. He carefully ensconced the principles of management within the broader principles of the Bible. He explored the role of the home in management development, and he dared to give us his opinions on the bringing up of children in the well-run home.

Looking back at my own successes and failures and those I have observed in others, I find they are quite consistent with the observations and warnings of Fayol. It is most interesting to me as a manager to see how I have measured up to Fayol's expectations. I must confess that if I ever found myself straying a distance from his principles, I would begin to think about a career change.

As managers, we know that the process of management is simple in concept, but almost impossible in execution. Fayol helped us by providing a compendium of what one should and should not do as a manager. I think most managers would agree that it contains little, if any, poor advice. So if Fayol suggested that some quality is "indispensable" to a manager, one ought to take it seriously.

Oh, that I might have more managers in my organization who possess the "indispensable" qualities Fayol described.

PAUL M. MONTRONE
Executive Vice President
The Signal Companies
Hampton, NH

FROM AN EXECUTIVE IN GOVERNMENT

This revision of *General and Industrial Management* by Henri Fayol represents far more than the rebirth of an out-of-print management classic. It is a reaffirmation of the relevance to modern industrial society of basic management principles articulated over half a century ago. Reading these principles reminds one of the phrase written in the original language of this book 80 years before the work appeared in English:

Plus ça change, plus c'est le même chose.
The more things change, the more they are the same.

Alphonse Karr, 1849

Fayol's work was the first to clearly establish that management is a process and that the process is applicable to all forms of organizations whether they deal with the marketplace, government, military, or social environment. The precepts remain timeless: they are not archaic curiosities applicable only to a bygone era. They are decidedly relevant to the management issues of today. Through this revision, Dr. Irwin Gray has expanded on Henri Fayol's message by adding explanatory material, by cutting away redundancies, and especially by restructuring the work to emphasize the points made by the author.

The practice of management, like the practice of music, sculpture, medicine, engineering, and most other endeavors, is an art. As such, the outstanding practitioners are those possessing innate talent, a characteristic present in some measure in everyone upon entering this world. Those with ample measures of talent improve their performance through study and practice. Those less gifted can aspire to successful performance through more hard work. So whatever the reader's innate management capabilities, he will undoubtedly find, in this book, things to be learned and concepts to improve his managerial performance.

Henri Fayol's classic, in this revised form, is recommended reading for all those who, in any way, must deal with the management of organizations—in short, all the nonhermits of society. The student just embarking on the examination of management concepts will discover not only conceptual gems, but an organizational framework for management that can serve well as a mental template for future studies. The functional specialist aspiring to a general management position can find a framework and substance to guide the necessary preparation. Top-level managers will probably be prompted by a refreshing review of the basic principles; they tend to be forgotten in the press of a busy career. Managers will also be renewing their knowledge of the all-important details of dealing with the body corporate, which are often overlooked under the crush of daily operations. It is those details that often make the difference between success and failure. Other readers should find the principles applicable to any activities in which resources and people are to be managed—whether in the home, professional or social organizations, or at the workplace.

In short, the timeless insight of Henri Fayol in combination with the modern extension provided by Dr. Gray should be valuable to all who take the time and trouble to think about what they have to do.

EDWARD A. WOLFF
NASA
Goddard Space Flight Center
Greenbelt, MD

General and Industrial
MANAGEMENT

1 Introduction

At the age of 75 Henri Fayol, the noted author of books and papers on mining, engineering, and administration, and the Managing Director of a huge combine, ensured his preeminence with the publication of *General and Industrial Management* in 1916. It was the first time that an individual of such rank had written down in a comprehensive and coherent manner the philosophy which guided him in building a rundown firm into one of the largest in the world. Unique when published, his views are now part of a larger mosaic of management theory covering every aspect of the operation of the modern concern. But those who study management have lost no respect for the continued integrity and applicability of his ideas, and they are still the "source" for the concept that the *process of management* is planning, organizing, coordinating, commanding, and controlling. And this process is exercised over the personnel of the firm according to a clear and definitive set of guiding principles. This book is a revised and updated presentation of Fayol's management theory. The revision recasts Fayol's ideas into a more modern format; the objective is to encourage contemporary management's reexamination, application, and further development of his classical concepts.

Our examination of Fayol's ideas will start by establishing their position within today's body of management theory. At the time of the publication of Fayol's work, it was complemented only by that of Frederick Winslow Taylor who viewed the firm from a position on the other end of the management spectrum. Today, the library of management theory examines, explains, and develops just about every known aspect of the management function in every known type of organization. Following the review of management schools, an overview of the layout and content of this book is provided. This chapter concludes with a discussion of how the book has been reorganized and the rationale for the way the revisions were made.

SCHOOLS OF MANAGEMENT THOUGHT

If management were a "hard science," the body of theory underlying it would be amenable to laboratory testing, replication, and expression in a unified way. There would be a single set of theories to form a "foundation" to the observations made in the laboratory, at work, or in other areas of life experiences. Management would have its equations, or dynamic principles, or even universal truths, which would be known or "sought" in much the way physicists, for example, are seeking a unified field theory—an elegant set of equations which would express the relationships of gravity fields with the electromagnetic fields of radio waves and light. Imagine the intellectual turmoil if researchers in management suspected even the possibility such equations could be established in their specialty!

Unfortunately, in the "soft sciences" we have no reason to expect that a single set of theories will ever be able to explain or predict phenomena. It is especially difficult to develop comprehensive theories in the management field, because it encompasses in umbrella fashion a variety of subspecialties each of which has its own theory base. It is unlikely that anyone will ever find a "unified management theory." Therefore, managers must be able to draw on a variety of theories in describing management phenomena, and they repeatedly face the question of which theory is appropriate in a given situation.

Let us, for brevity and ease of exposition, view the variety of management theories as encompassing five major subspecialties and examine how each affects our understanding of the field. We label these the economic, production, governance, human relations, and cybernetics "schools of thought."

The Economic School

This school is illustrated by the economic drive behind the formation of the Hanseatic league, an economic confederation of north German towns in the thirteenth century. The towns combined in a permanent union for the defense of their commerce on the North Sea and for the control of the Baltic. Members of the league were engaged in common trade or other economic activities, lent one another moral support, and performed such business functions as accounting, sales, manufacturing, and shipping. While the league carried with it political and military defense overtones, there is no doubt that the main unifying impetus for its formation was the protection of economic aims, and all other considerations were ruthlessly subordinated to them. This primacy of economic aims, as opposed to all others, made the league a pioneering entity in business and its activities provide one category, or school, of management thinking. Fayol, in his work, showed no antipathy to economic thinking. Indeed, he recognized quite early that the commercial activities of a firm were key to its existence, and they were accorded prominence in his theory.

The Production School of Management

In this management school, the focus is on operating efficiency—output must be maximized in relation to the input resources consumed. The pioneers in this branch of management include many people, from the inventors of the cotton gin and the machinery that made possible the mass production of textiles, to the singular genius represented by Eli Whitney. He promoted the concept of interchangeable parts and thereby laid the foundation for mass production. Whitney made use of the whole body of existing mechanical and industrial engineering sciences to set up a production line, make the individual parts, check their characteristics, and assemble them into the finished products. This approach demonstrated that efficiency in the use of resources was a key to success. Fayol also saw the need for making the production process as efficient in its use of resources as the sciences could make them. He called for the proper training of engineers to provide dynamic leadership of the "works," and the resulting economies, efficiencies, and general production knowhow were the keys to the rejuvenation of the company he led.

The Governance School of Management

In this school of management thought, the focus is on the organizational structure and the principles by which it is "governed." The structure is carefully defined, the lines of authority and responsibility are delineated, and rules of law, policy, and protocol are established from the top management levels down to the personnel who actually make, ship, and sell the product. Henri Fayol is credited with the role of pioneer in this school of thought, as his "process of management" focuses on planning, organizing, coordinating, commanding, and controlling. His 14 principles—including those of equity, unity of command, and scalar chain—are a part of this school of management thought.

The Human Relations School of Management

This school owes its origin to Elton Mayo, who pioneered the concern for an organization's "human relations." In Mayo's view, self-actualization of the employee—expressed as growth, professional accomplishment, and development into "the person of one's dreams"—is the key to an organization's accomplishments. The 1923 experiments at the Hawthorne Works of Western Electric supported Mayo's theories. The employees' feelings were shown to be of greater weight in levels of productivity than the purely industrial engineering principles of table layout, lighting, and other mechanical factors. Under this school of thinking, management pursues a policy in which the attitudes and morale of employees are paramount, and methods are adjusted to provide the best psychological environment.

The Cybernetic School of Management

This school is of relatively recent origin and was probably first identified by Norbert Weiner, the father of "cybernetics" (from the Greek "cyber," meaning steersman). Weiner pointed to the increased availability of information and the use of decision-making processes as keys to the survival of an organization and to its "adaptability" as a focal measure of its operations. He believed that the challenge of the future was for managers to learn to 1) establish information systems, 2) generate the appropriate data, 3) separate applicable information from the massive flow that technology and systems can create, 4) identify the decisions needed, and 5) make decisions according to carefully established rules. A firm that can adapt (measure its output, provide feedback to the input, and change the output as needed) is one that will avoid organizational fractionalization, obsolescence, or economic destruction. Such a firm is best able to survive the massive changes taking place in society. Management is seen as a "steersman," guiding the organization along the self-adjusting path. The body of cybernetic theory is being increasingly applied to explain why certain organizations succeed where others fail. Parts of Fayol's work encompass cybernetic concepts of control—the functions of monitoring and correcting.

MULTIDIMENSIONAL THINKING

The mind sets of managers often reflect the background specialties from which they achieved promotion into management. Engineers tend to make decisions in which the engineering production-oriented approach receives priority when other considerations should have been preeminent. A financial executive focuses on the cash-flow aspects of a decision and makes evaluations accordingly. People tend to revert, unless specially trained to do otherwise, to one school of thought on which to base their decisions, the one through which they have developed their careers and which they find most familiar, comfortable, and secure. Such one-dimensional thinking is the hallmark of the mediocre manager because a decision made from the wrong theoretical base is a decision that will have to be remade. A problem solved with a wrong or incomplete theoretical base will have to be resolved when it comes back again—and it most assuredly will do so, in a more intractable form than when first encountered. The problem will require more resources and more effort to solve, and will have done greater damage on its reappearance than if it had been dealt with properly when first encountered.

The better managers are wholly conversant with the broad range of management thinking. They appreciate the wide scope of the economic, production, human, and other organizational considerations involved in even the least significant situations. They are prepared to turn to any one or combination of the theories if that is what is best for solving their problems. But the top-flight managers go beyond even this. The best managers can not only pick out the best schools, or combination of schools, and use them to map their response, but they go one step further, on paper, before implementation. They assess the consequences of the potential decisions by checking their implications with regard to all the other schools of management thought. How will this "production decision" affect the organization structure? Human relations? Information flow? What will be harmed? What will the benefits be? If it appears that a decision made in accordance with the most appropriate school will yield harm in terms of another, then the decision is modified, the approach is changed, or other adjustments are made as necessary. The best managers keep themselves current and open to varying viewpoints. Not only can they apply the precepts of each school effectively, but they can evaluate how a new development or approach will affect their organizations from the vantage points of every school of management thought.

THIS BOOK: THE GOVERNANCE SCHOOL

In 1916, when Fayol's examination of the firm "from the top down" was first published in a French mining journal, it broke new ground. Management theory was nonexistent at the time, and Fayol's exposition on the process of management, as well as his principles for directing the body corporate, were a welcome addition to management knowledge. Fayol identified the manager's job as carrying out a process which consisted of five parts: planning for the organization, organizing it, coordinating its operating parts, commanding it, and controlling it. In more detailed terms, management was responsible for 1) defining what it wanted to accomplish, 2) creating the lines of authority and responsibility along which the orders flow to start the work, 3) issuing the commands by which the entire organization is set in motion, 4) establishing the sequence of the work, and 5) continuously monitoring and correcting the work once it had begun.

The key element in all this was not directly stated in Fayol's work, but nevertheless comes through with strength: the objective of a firm is to produce a product or service and successfully deliver it to its market or constituency. It is this product or service which justifies the flow of revenue to the organization, be it an industrial works, nonprofit service, or government organization.

The mechanism through which management achieves its aims is the "body corporate." This is a carefully considered translation of Fayol's term "corps social" and refers to the entire body of personnel engaged in the totality of an organization's activities. Fayol used the somewhat unusual term "corps social" because of the implied biological metaphor: he wished to emphasize the structure as distinct from the process of organization. The process of management is applied to the body corporate, which in turn does the work to produce and deliver the product or service. Fayol provided a series of principles by which management should work with its body corporate to achieve organizational goals. These principles are intended to guide management in carrying out the process—in motivating, rewarding, and disciplining the body corporate. The process of management is the tool: Fayol's principles tell how to apply the tool.

ORGANIZATION OF THIS REVISION

Appendixes I and II provide notes on Henri Fayol and on how his management classic came to be written.

Fayol's original book presents barriers to the reader in terms of its organization (the ideas are scattered), a good deal of parochial and dated comment about the French government, ideas about education which are completely outmoded, and the writing style used. The English translation done in 1929 did not much improve upon the original French and introduced difficulties of its own—it became more archaic with the passage of time and in comparison to later management classics. The present edition of Fayol's book has been extensively restructured so that its presentation of ideas follows a more logical order. The book starts with Fayol's definition of management and the major activities that comprise the industrial undertaking, with appropriate comments on other types of organizations as well. This is followed by separate chapters covering the component parts of the management process including planning, organizing, coordinating, commanding, and controlling. Next is a chapter explaining Fayol's 14 principles and their function in the carrying out of the management process. The book closes with an analysis of the abilities required of the manager, in particular the need for "multidimensional" thinking, and comments on how this type of thinking is developed. Finally, Fayol's advice to new graduates is presented.

In the preparation of this revision, a guiding philosophy has been to present Fayol's ideas as he himself might have presented them if he had been writing in more modern times. The revision, although it contains extensive structural changes, still retains nearly all the ideas and special terminology of the original classic. The main changes, which were designed to make the book more organized and readable, were the following:

1) Several concepts that later research or practice has shown to be wrong or totally inappropriate to modern management concepts were omitted or revised as necessary.

2) Supplemental material in key areas was added so that the ideas Fayol presented remain coherent "wholes" in light of modern theory and practice. The ideas were whole when Fayol wrote from the vantage point of his times; they should, it was felt, remain so in this revised edition. Some notes to guide the reader on what was added and deleted are included in Appendix V.

3) The material has been resequenced within the chapters and from chapter to chapter so that ideas on particular topics are more integrated and are presented in one place—with less scatter.

4) Sentence structures have been revised to permit easier and faster comprehension.

The revision has been done with an appreciation for Henri Fayol and his times, for the nature and theoretical weaknesses of management practices then, and for the pioneering scope of his work. The more modern setting helps illustrate the extent to which Fayol's ideas are as current today as they were in 1916. He looked at the organization from the "top down" even as others, such as America's Frederick Winslow Taylor, examined the work of the firm from the "bottom up." While Fayol showed the organization operating from the chief executive down, Taylor and other authors of the day were conducting time and motion studies of machines, workers, and processes. Fayol was the first author to 1) identify management as a process, 2) break that process down into a series of logical subparts, and 3) lay out a series of principles by which management could apply the process to make best use of the organization's personnel.

The basic concepts of Henri Fayol have stood the test of time. His principle of discipline, for example, would do credit to any modern university code of conduct, any business, or any church group. And the same could be said for his thoughts on equity, order, initiative, and the remainder of the 14 principles. It is hoped that the present edition of *General and Industrial Management* not only will aid managers who from time to time want to refresh their thinking with the basics, but will cause them to realize the comprehensive nature and current applicability of Fayol's thinking.

2 Definition of Management

All activities to which organizational undertakings give rise can be divided into the following six functions:

1) Technical (engineering, production, manufacture, adaptation).
2) Commercial (buying, selling, exchange).
3) Financial (search for and optimum use of capital).
4) Security (protection of assets and personnel).
5) Accounting (stocktaking, balance sheets, costs, statistics).
6) Managerial (planning, organizing, commanding, coordinating, controlling).

Whether the undertaking is simple or complex, large or small, these six essential functions are always present. Each function encompasses a wide variety of activities. The first five functions and their related activities are well known—a few words will be enough to demarcate their respective spheres—but the managerial function will be discussed at greater length in Chapters 3–7.

TECHNICAL FUNCTION

The number, variety, and importance of technical activities, the fact that products of every kind (material or intellectual) originate with technical personnel—all these factors contribute to making the technical function, and in consequence, technical ability, extremely important. Nevertheless, the technical function is not always the central one. Even in industrial undertakings, there are circumstances where one of the other functions may exercise a much greater influence over the running of the business than does the technical function. Furthermore, it is important to note that the six essential functions are closely interdependent; the technical function, for instance, cannot exist without finance, commerce, accounting, security, and management.

COMMERCIAL FUNCTION

The prosperity of an organization—be it a business, a foundation, or even a government agency—often will depend as much on the commercial as on the technical function. For a product or service not to "sell" means ruin. Knowledge of buying and selling is just as important as knowledge of efficient production. However, commercial ability requires not only the acumen of how to convert prospects to customers, but a thorough knowledge of the market, the competition, and long-term foresight with respect to both.

Finally, when goods or services are sold by one division to another within the same concern, the commercial function must see to it that the transfer prices do not shortchange the selling division (and unduly benefit the buyer) or overcharge a captive buyer (and unduly benefit the seller). Such practices distort the costs of goods sold to the ultimate markets of the firm and have consequent impacts on divisional earnings statements. Management cannot operate properly when such basic operating statements do not reflect a true state of affairs.

FINANCIAL FUNCTION

Nothing happens within an organization without the financial function playing a part. Capital is required for such elements as, for example, personnel, plant, tools, raw materials, dividends, development, and reserves. Shrewd financial management is necessary to obtain capital, to make optimum use of available funds, and to avoid foolhardy commitments. Many potentially prosperous enterprises die because they suffer from lack of money. And any reform or improvement in the way an organization is operating is impossible without finances or credit. An essential condition of success is to keep constant watch over the financial position of the business.

Internally, one of the major financial tools is the budget. Although a budget may be recognized as a detailed financial planning tool from firm to firm, in fact there are widely different orientations toward its use and preparation. A "control orientation" is said to be predominant when managerial emphasis is on holding an agency, a department, or a function in an organization to a preset expenditure ceiling. A "planning orientation" emphasizes the determination of objectives, the evaluation of alternatives, and the authorization of the financing of selected programs. A "management orientation" stresses tracking of the resources needed, obtained, and used vis-à-vis the attainment of the organization's objectives.

Externally, the financial concerns of an organization will extend to its balance sheets (assets versus liabilities), its costs (of goods sold, services rendered, overhead), its revenues, and its earnings. With regard to earnings, the fact that a firm is "making money" is not, by itself, sufficient to assure its continuing existence. As those with a "quality of earnings" orientation have pointed out, a firm's financial strength is also reflected in its cash flow, its stability (or growth), and the degree to which its success stems from real factors rather than from the artificial effects of inflation.

The financial function is also concerned with preserving the cash assets of the firm against loss of value due to inflation, international currency problems, and payment of taxes that the organization could legally avoid. To this end, financial managers will carefully manage the firm's debts, invest the firm's surplus cash wisely (even for very short periods), maintain prudent accounts-receivable and payable policies, engage in systematic and timely repatriation of foreign earnings, and engage competent counsel in handling the tax situation.

SECURITY FUNCTION

The traditional view of security confines its attention to the physical assets of the organization and to the immediate protection of its personnel. In this view, the objectives are to safeguard property and persons against theft, fire, and flood, to ward off sabotage and felonies, and to avoid all disturbances that are liable to endanger the progress and even the life of the business. Security may be provided by "the master's eye," the watchdog of the one-man business, by the police or army in the case of the state, by the security force of a corporation, or through the use of sophisticated security systems necessary to the protection of an organization's assets. All measures conferring security upon the undertaking and requisite peace of mind on the personnel are regarded as part of this function.

However, the security function of an organization is best viewed in a broader sense: those responsible for security protect the firm against all forms of threat to its assets and personnel. A major component of security is risk management, which involves exposure identification, risk evaluation, risk control (eliminating hazards, minimizing the effects of those which cannot be eliminated, warning against the remainder), and risk financing (such as absorbing losses, self-insuring, outside insuring, sinking funds, and transferring risk to a supplier or client through contracts).

Newer approaches to security involve broad definitions of "property." The property of an organization may be defined as being not only physical but intellectual as well. Quite frequently, the greatest danger to a firm lies in the loss of intellectual property, a loss that the firm may attempt to prevent through patent protection, trade-secret protection, signed agreements (nondisclosures) with key personnel, and access to its innermost secrets on a strictly "need to know" basis. An assault on a firm's intellectual property can come through organized spying by foreign nationals, the purchase of secrets from suborned officials of the firm, the carrying away of secrets in the minds of departing employees, and even theft of key drawings and designs from computer memory banks. Such theft, in terms of its impact on the firm, often dwarfs the more mundane thefts of the firm's physical property. Because intellectual property can be a firm's most valuable asset, security in this broader sense has become much more important to management in the latter half of the twentieth century than ever before. Management must now be aware of any personnel and physical problems, technical deficiencies, or weak points in the functioning of the organization which might tempt key personnel to remove the intellectual property of the firm. Once removed, such property is difficult to recapture. The firm seeking compensation for such a loss may face a long, difficult, and generally very expensive court process in which there is a high risk that nothing will be won.

ACCOUNTING FUNCTION

The accounting function is the visual organ of businesses. At any given moment, it must afford an accurate, precise picture of the economic position of the concern and likely future trends. An efficient accounting system that offers a clear idea of the firm's condition is a powerful managerial instrument. For this group of activities, as for the others, competence in performance is assured only by intensive training in a broad range of areas. They may be ancillary to the main duties, but are still relevant to the documentation or measurement of the firm's activities; included is an in-depth understanding of the nature of the products or services from which the firm generates its revenues.

The ability of the computer to absorb vast amounts of data and keep track of numerous financial, sales, and other measures has resulted in the creation of complex management information systems (MIS). Because accounting generates the numbers used by the systems, many organizations place MIS under the accounting department.

MANAGERIAL FUNCTION

None of the preceding functions encompasses the drawing up of the broad plan of how the business will operate, assembling the personnel, or coordinating and harmonizing all of the organization's efforts and activities. Strictly speaking, the latter functions do not fall within the province of those managers who control technical, commercial, financial, security, or accounting functions. They make up another group of activities, which have somewhat ill-defined attributes and boundaries and are usually referred to by the term "management." It is generally agreed that planning, organizing, coordinating, and controlling are basic management activities. The activity of command is sometimes accorded separate status; management and command are regarded as complementary functions. Here, command is one of the activities included as a part of the management function for the following reasons:

1) The managerial responsibilities of selecting and training personnel and setting up the overall organization are very much concerned with command.

2) Most principles of command are principles of management; management and command are very closely linked. In order to facilitate study, there is reason to consider command as one of the activities making up the function of management.

3) There is a clear link between those aspects of management which are executed on paper and those aspects which involve putting things into motion—getting the action started and seeing the action through to completion. In war, the act of command is the one by which troops quit sharpening their swords and begin using them.

Therefore, the following definition has been adopted: to manage is to plan, organize, coordinate, command, and control. Each of these subactivities can, in turn, be defined as follows:

1) To plan: examine the future and lay out the actions to be taken.

2) To organize: lay out the lines of authority and responsibility; build up the dual structure, material and human, of the undertaking.

3) To coordinate: lay out the timing and sequencing of activities; bind together, unify, and harmonize all activities and efforts.

4) To command: put the plan into action; set the work in operation.

5) To control: monitor and correct; see that everything occurs in conformity with established rules and expressed command.

Management, thus understood, is neither an exclusive privilege nor a particular responsibility of the head of an organization or its senior members; it is an activity spread across all members of the "body corporate"— the total personnel structure of the organization. The managerial function is quite distinct from the other five essential functions; it supersedes them and, in effect, directs them toward the achievement of the objectives of the undertaking. The managerial function seeks to derive optimum advantage from all available resources and to assure the smooth working of the six essential functions including the managerial function itself.

3 Planning

The maxim "managing means looking ahead" gives some idea of the importance attached to planning in the business world. If foresight is not the whole of management, it is at least an essential part of it. To foresee, in this context, means both to assess the future and to make provisions for it; that is, for the manager, foreseeing is an essential part of action. Planning is manifested on a variety of occasions and in a variety of ways. In developing a plan of action, the manager must include the overall result envisaged, results expected for each of the major stages in accomplishment, the general methodology to be employed in the execution of the plans, and a general layout of the timing of actions and expected results. The plan is a future picture wherein events appear progressively less distinct as they become more distant from the present, and it is the basic means for guiding the business over a managerially defined period.

The plan of action rests 1) on the firm's resources (such as buildings, tools, raw materials, personnel, productive capacity, sales outlets, and public relations), 2) on the nature and importance of work in progress, and 3) on future trends, which depend on technical, commercial, financial, and other conditions that are changeable and can never be wholly predicted. The preparation of the plan of action is one of the most difficult and most important matters of every business and brings into play all departments and all functions, especially the management function. The execution of the managerial function is, in effect, the process whereby the manager takes the initiative for the plan of action, indicating its objective and scope, fixing the share of each department in the communal task, coordinating the parts, and harmonizing the whole. In other words, the manager decides the line of conduct to be followed by the enterprise. In this line of conduct it is imperative that nothing should clash with the principles of good management and that specific actions being planned should facilitate application of those principles. Therefore, besides the diverse technical, commercial, financial, and other abilities necessary if the plan of action is to be successful, there must be added considerable general managerial ability.

GENERAL FEATURES OF A GOOD PLAN OF ACTION

No one disputes the usefulness of a plan of action. Before taking action it is important to know what is possible and what is wanted. The absence of a plan often results in hesitation, false steps, and untimely changes of direction—occurrences that can cause weaknesses in or even disaster for a business. While few would argue that a plan of action is indispensable to the success of an organization, choosing the specific plan to implement can be extremely difficult. There are plans and plans; there are simple ones, complex ones, concise ones, detailed ones, long- or short-term ones; there are those studied with meticulous attention, those treated lightly; there are good, bad, and indifferent ones. How are the good ones to be singled out from among the others?

The ultimate outcome of a plan, in terms of the services it has rendered to the firm, is the only thing that finally determines its true value. Yet even when the verdict of success or failure is in, one cannot make an absolute statement that a plan was a good or a bad one. Perhaps the plan was applied inadequately or perhaps the firm succeeded despite the plan. Experience does yield some valuable lessons, however. There are certain broad characteristics of plans which appear crucial to their success.

One such characteristic is a plan's unity. Only one basic plan can be put into operation at a time; two different plans would mean duality, confusion, and disorder. A basic plan must often be divided into several parts: in large concerns, technical, commercial, and financial subplans are found alongside the general plan, or else there may be a specific subplan for each department. But all of these subplans are linked and welded, so as to add up to only one overall plan; every modification brought to bear on any one of the subplans is given expression in the whole plan. A plan, if it is to set forth guiding actions for the firm, must also have continuity. Although the limitations of human foresight necessarily set bounds to the duration of plans, the manager should try to anticipate as far into the future as possible. In order to have no break in the plan's guiding action, a second plan should follow immediately upon the first, a third upon the second, and so on. In large businesses, the annual plan is generally considered the operating plan. Other plans of shorter or longer term operate simultaneously with the annual plan, always in close accord.

Next, the plan should have enough flexibility to bend before whatever adjustments management finds it advisable to introduce, whether they are due to pressure of circumstances or any other reasons. New developments in the firm's environment, not rigid specifications of a plan that has become obsolete, must be the law to which management bows. A plan should also have as much accuracy as is compatible with the fact that unknown factors will always bear on the fate of a concern. It is usually possible to establish the guidelines for imminent action fairly accurately, while a more general indication will have to suffice for remote activities. By the time remote activities have become imminent ones, management will generally have obtained sufficient enlightenment to set forth proposed lines of action more precisely. When unknown factors occupy a very large place in a plan, preciseness is sacrificed and the concern is embarked on a true "venture" with all the risk that the term implies.

Unity, continuity, flexibility, and accuracy—such are the broad features of a good plan of action. The more specific features of a plan will turn 1) on the nature, priorities, and condition of the business for which the plan is drawn up, 2) on long-range predictions for the industry and economy, 3) on the intuitions of key thinkers, and 4) on strategic analyses conducted by staff groups charged with assessing the relevant parameters and determining how their findings can be incorporated into the outlines of the plan. Management may also wish to evaluate its tentative plan in comparison to completed plans that are recognized as having been effective, such as plans used by client firms or suppliers and even the announced plans of competitors.

In each case, management should carefully assess whether the elements of its own plans and those of plans used by others are truly comparable. When this caveat is observed, it can be very useful to seek models in business practice, after the fashion of the architect who has a building to construct. There is no lack of good plans, most well-run businesses provide at least a few excellent examples. Something new can often be learned from the methods adopted by others. It is useful to examine the various procedures involved in drawing up a set of business operating plans. Plans evolve from the general to the specific; from the long-term to the short-term; from outlines of broad needs and corporate "directions" to the specific projects that must be undertaken. As an example, consider the sequence of events leading to the construction of a large metallurgical works. Upper management is alerted to the need for new capacity by its own staff and by its system of tracking past, present, and probable future events in the industry—anything that can possibly relate to the selling, making, or use of steel products. Upper management's system for recording such information integrates contributions made by senior members of the firm, by the operating personnel, by outside sources, and by the specialists engaged for the express purpose of analyzing relevant events.

A survey is undertaken that is concerned with each and every part of the business. The survey results show the firm's and the industry's situation in the past, present, and probable future. The historical part of the survey deals with the considerations that led to the formation of the undertaking, the internal and external changes that have taken place since that time, and the results that have been achieved. The present situation is shown in full detail as to the resources and needs of the undertaking, looked at from every point of view. The picture of the probable future is arrived at by taking into account the past and the present prevailing, economic, political, and social circumstances that affect the industry and the surrounding economy. From this survey it is possible to develop a complete picture of how the firm should develop over the next ten years or more. Questions that the survey can answer, in part, are what types of products will be in demand, what sales volumes can be reasonably expected, what prices can be charged, what competitive materials will become available, what trend costs must follow, where will new markets come from, and where should the firm be active? If such projections are "overlaid" with a picture of the present shape of the firm, the needed plan of action becomes sharply focused. Management can compare "what is presently available" with "what will be needed" for every department or activity, such as research (new processes needed to deal with the newest materials or to achieve cost reductions), capacity planning, transportation planning, supply planning, and sales planning. Such strategic thinking leads to 1) identification of long-term needs, 2) translation of needs into specific activities, 3) further translation into resources to be allocated, 4) establishment of timetables for execution, 5) issuance of the work orders, and 6) the actual construction of the new metallurgical works. Research, capacity planning, or any other activity should not be happening by chance unless truly fortuitous events have taken place. The large firm cannot, as a regular way of doing business, afford to expend massive resources responding frequently to chance events.

While it is not within the scope of this discussion to cover all the details of planning that would be involved in such an endeavor, below are some bare outlines of how planning might be structured by a mining and metallurgical concern.

THE ROLES OF STRATEGIC ANALYSIS AND DIVISIONAL PLANNING GROUPS

Assume the company includes several divisions and employs about 20,000 employees in widely separated facilities. Company planning is begun by a strategic analysis/long-range planning group charged with establishing where the company is to go over the next ten years. The group is charged with predicting what markets, supplies, and a host of other international and domestic factors will be like by the end of the decade, and with determining how the firm is to evolve to meet the challenges that become evident. The group is to deliver to the next planning units a set of assumptions, guiding principles, and long-range targets that are to be proportionately met under shorter-term plans. This same group, upon completion of this initial assignment, then becomes the five-year planning group. In effect, it decides on the proportionate share of the ten-year results to be achieved in five years and on the basic structures that should be set in place during those five years to assure that plans in the subsequent five years can move ahead on schedule. That is, the planners determine which research groups should be functioning and what objectives they should have, which types of organizational structure should be established, and which types of financing should be arranged. The product of their work is a set of ten-year overall strategic assumptions and a five-year strategic plan.

The major divisional units of the firm are staffed with planning committees. Each committee is charged with deriving a five-year plan for its division that dovetails with the five-year plan on the corporate level and is charged with producing yearly subplans divided, in turn, into monthly operational projections. The committees at the divisional level are, in addition, responsible for certain special plans involving the direction of projects or activities that require long incubation periods, and are responsible for certain standing plans that serve as guides to action in cases when specific events occur (for example, the company becomes the target of a product liability suit; a major asset is lost in a natural disaster; a portion of its executive staff leaves; or a major competitive challenge develops). The plans prepared by all of these committees are drawn up in such a way that they merge hierarchically into a single well-documented plan that serves as a guide for the whole concern.

The Ten-Year Plan

Our rapidly changing technological world discourages some firms from doing long-term planning because they maintain it is totally impossible to envision what the world will be like in ten years. Such firms prefer shorter planning periods such as five years at maximum. However, larger technologically oriented firms are increasingly vulnerable to fast-moving competition in their various product lines, both internationally as well as domestically. Management should protect the company by staying ahead of competitors instead of waiting until threats materialize and then simply reacting. The latter course of action could result in major damage to a firm's standing in the marketplace or even the obsolescence of an entire line of products.

Those responsible for strategic thinking, in seeking to establish "what will be needed" at given points in time, can project a firm's activities into the future by studying previous trends and conducting diligent research on the increasing technological capabilities that customers or clients will be demanding in the future. Many trends are relatively clear, such as those in health care, home entertainment, and foods. In areas where trends are well recognized, there is little excuse for the firm not to establish a set of assumptions about the nature of its business and forecasts that are applicable to the next ten years. General projections are then translated into specific operational plans by projecting such elements as the nature of the facilities needed to supply the products, the personnel needed to staff those facilities, the finances needed to support them, and so on. Then, the projections are made even more specific by tying them into what the firm is currently doing and the resources it is now using to supply its markets; how can these be converted to meet the future demands? Management lays out a general blueprint for the types of actions to be taken, signposts to watch for, and various elements to keep under consideration as shorter-term subplans are drawn up. The ten-year assumptions, dealing with conditions in the relatively distant future, are the foundation for the assumptions of the five-year plans, which, in turn, lay the bases for shorter-term plans. In many firms, the ten-year projections are rolling plans: they are upgraded each year for the following ten years on the basis of the latest results and newly revised assumptions about the future.

The Five-Year Plans

The five-year plan, which is built on the general outlines of the ten-year assumptions and projections, is frequently considered to be *the strategic plan* of a firm. This plan lays out in specific terms what the firm anticipates to be its long-term financing, long-term technical directions, long-term product lines, and all derivative parameters. The strategic plan answers the question, "Where do we want to be in five years?" And, in effect, it tells the firm what it should do to get there. This plan may be laid out by function, product line, or divisional jurisdiction within the firm. It will contain 1) a full description of the external and internal conditions expected to affect the firm's operations, 2) the objectives that the firm has established for the ten-year period, 3) the results expected over the five-year period in relation to the ten-year targets, and 4) details on where and how the resources are to be phased into the ongoing operations to assure that the results are attained as projected.

Yearly Subplans

Each year, two months before the end of the budgetary period, a general report is drawn up of the work that is expected to have been accomplished by the end of the period. These projections offer concrete figures for key indicators of the firm's operating health, such as projected return on investment, projected total production, projected costs, and projected sales. The report expresses the projections in absolute terms, as trends, as ratios (such as compensation to sales or inventory to sales), as comparisons of internal measures to equivalents outside the firm, or as variances from previously established norms. The report also includes projections of the key indicators for the next year. These projections, when they include summaries of internal and external conditions that are anticipated over the new budgetary period, may be labeled forecasts. Adding the details of everything that must be done to achieve the projected results—such as times to start, resources needed, and lines of authority and responsibility—results in the construction of a complete plan.

In all the assumptions and projections in the report, reference is made to the five-year plan and to the expected percentage of the five-year plan that is to be achieved in the following year. The report also sets forth the expected percentage of resources that will be consumed in achieving the desired results and enumerates the projects that will have to be set in place during the coming year to assure continued progress. In addition, the plan shows such details as training needed for personnel, expected technical achievements, and the manner in which the firm plans to improve its standing in the marketplace.

A suggested breakdown of the yearly, five-year, and ten-year plans would include, among others, the following sections:

PLAN CONTENTS: A MINING AND METALLURGY FIRM

Technical Section

- Mining rights. Physical facilities.
- Mining processes. Manufacturing processes.
- New workings. Improvements.
- Research. Design. Pollution control.
- Maintenance of plant and buildings.
- Production costs.

Commercial Section

- Sales outlets.
- Types of marketable goods.
- Legal services. Contracts.
- Customers (importance and credit standing).
- Selling price. International and domestic conditions.
- Prices of direct substitutes for our products.
- Prices of indirect substitutes. Prices of complementary products.
- Competition.
- Government actions.

Financial Section

- Capital. Loans. Deposits.
- Investments.
- Circulating assets—supplies in hand, goods in process, liquid assets.
- Finished goods. Accounts receivable. Accounts payable.
- Reserves and sundry appropriations.
- Wages, salaries. Suppliers.
- Sinking funds. Dividends. Bankers.
- Capital. Depreciation. Taxes.
- International transfers. Currency (restrictions and fluctuations).
- Stock ratios. Share price. Stability/growth of earnings.

Accounting

- Balance sheet. Profit and loss.
- Taxes.
- Costs. Ratios. Statistics.
- Management information systems.

- Risk elimination.
- Risk minimization.
- Warnings.
- Works claims. Accident prevention. Health maintenance.
- Insurance.
- Protection of intellectual and physical property.

Management

- Full set of plans drawn up.
- Organization structure and charts.
- Command outlines/guidelines.
- Coordination mechanisms, milestones, timing.
- Apparatus for maintenance of the control function.

Special Plans

In contrast to activities whose full cycle may be ten years or more, there are activities that are embarked upon fairly suddenly in response to changing business conditions. Such activities may be covered in special subplans that become part of the yearly, five-year, and ten-year plans.

While a firm may have a multitude of subplans, it should always be kept in mind that the well-run firm has only one plan and all the others are, effectively, component parts of that plan. The ten-year, five-year, yearly, and special plans when merged and harmonized constitute the firm's general plan.[1] The various subparts of the plan should be prepared with meticulous care by special planning groups, regional or divisional committees, and departmental management; they should then be revised and completed by general management, and, finally, should be submitted for scrutiny and approval to the managing directors or their delegates. The resulting plan serves as a guide, directive, and law for the whole staff.

The planning process described here does, necessarily, have some shortcomings, although they are very slight compared to the advantages offered. Let us glance at these advantages and shortcomings.

ADVANTAGES AND SHORTCOMINGS OF THE PLANNING PROCESS

1) As members of a firm study the resources available, investigate future possibilities, and consider what means will be used to attain com-

---

[1]In addition, monthly, weekly, and daily plans are in use in most businesses. These, like longer-term plans, are aimed at marking out beforehand the lines of action judged to be most conducive to the firm's success. Such plans should be made available early enough so that the personnel involved will have time to prepare for their implementation.

pany objectives, informative data come from all departmental heads. Each person, within the framework of his mandate, brings to this study the value of his experience and insights together with recognition of the responsibility that will fall upon him in implementing the plan. These are excellent conditions for ensuring that no resource will be neglected, that future possibilities will be prudently and courageously assessed, and that means will be appropriate to ends. When a firm's planning capabilities are fully harnessed through the involvement of all key personnel, the company is better able to tackle current problems confidently and to align all its forces against accidents and surprises that may occur.

2) Compiling the annual plan is always a delicate operation; the process may be especially lengthy and laborious when done for the first time. But each repetition brings some simplification, and when the plan has become a habit, the toil and difficulties are greatly reduced. Furthermore, repetition of the planning process brings more and more interesting facts to light. The experiences of those who executed the most recent plan, the new and creative insights developed, the indispensable comparisons between predicted and actual facts, the recognition of mistakes made and successes attained, the search for means of repeating the successes and avoiding the failures—all go to make each new plan a work of increasing interest and increasing usefulness. And as the personnel do this work, their experience increases in value from year to year, becoming considerably superior to what it was in the beginning. In truth, this result does not stem solely from the use of planning: everything going on in the firm has combined to improve the individual managerial abilities. A well thought out plan is rarely found apart from sound organizational, command, coordination, and control practices. The planning process exerts an influence on all the other managerial activities, and vice versa.

3) A business without a plan may engage in unconnected activities that do not form a logical sequence, and may be constantly threatened by unwarranted changes of direction. The slightest contrary wind can turn from its course a boat that is unfitted to resist. When something serious occurs, management, under the influence of a disturbance that may prove to be only transitory, may decide on a change of course that will later be regretted. Only a program carefully pondered at an undisturbed time will permit management to maintain a clear view of the future, and when danger does arise, to concentrate maximum possible intellectual ability and material resources on dealing with it.

In fact, it is in difficult moments, above all, that a plan is necessary. Even the best of plans cannot anticipate all possible occurrences, but good plans do take into account as many unexpected events as possible and prepare the weapons that may be needed at moments of surprise. A plan not only protects the business against undesirable changes of course in response to grave events, but also protects the business against subjective or whimsical behaviors on the part of higher management and against deviations, perhaps nearly imperceptible at first, that end by deflecting the firm from its objectives.

CONDITIONS AND QUALITIES ESSENTIAL FOR
DRAWING UP A GOOD PLAN OF ACTION

A good plan of action facilitates the optimal utilization of the firm's resources and helps management to choose the best methods for attaining its objectives. Such a plan reduces hesitancy, false steps, and unwarranted changes of course, and it enhances the abilities of key personnel. It is a precious managerial instrument.

Therefore, one may ask why such an instrument has not been developed everywhere and to the furthest extent possible. The reason for this is that the compilation of such a plan will proceed well only in an atmosphere where certain qualities and conditions, rarely found in combination, are prevalent. In order for a good plan to be compiled, the personnel in charge should

1) be skilled in the art of handling personnel;
2) have considerable energy;
3) have a measure of moral courage;
4) have some continuity of tenure;
5) be competent in the specialized requirements of the business;
6) have general business experience and ability to generate creative ideas.

Skill in Handling Personnel

In a large firm the majority of departmental managers not only carry out their everyday responsibilities, but assist in establishing the general working climate of that business. Whether it manifests itself in the specific treatment accorded a single employee's problems or in the equity which rules all interactions with subordinates, the departmental managers play the key role in the physical manifestations of that climate. Such activity does not carry any special recognition for them nor does it normally carry any special remuneration. So, higher management must establish the conditions which inspire the loyal and active cooperation of the departmental heads. Their superior, in turn, must be an individual who will stand by his subordinates and who fears neither the trouble that may result from his stand nor the responsibility of taking it. When a manager, at any level, has perfected the art of handling personnel, this is apparent from the keenness of his subordinates and the confidence of his superiors.

Energy

All types of planning, ranging from the ten-year variety to special planning, demand a high energy level. Management must then exercise constant vigilance over the implementation of these plans and should demand equivalent levels of effort on the part of subordinates. Management should be prepared to help troubled groups with temporary manpower and the application of creative problem-solving talent, but these efforts should not dilute the application of effort by those who hold the primary responsibilities. It must be kept in mind that the application of productive effort on all levels is what determines the success or failure of the enterprise.

Moral Courage

Even the best thought out plan is never carried out in exactly the way envisioned by the planners. Forecasts are not prophecies: their function is simply to minimize the unknown factors as much as possible. Nevertheless, those who see a plan fail often judge the planners harshly. The public generally—and even shareholders who are supposed to be well informed about how businesses are run—are not kindly disposed toward a manager who has raised unfulfilled hopes or allowed others to raise such hopes. Therefore, planners must reconcile their desire to be prudent—that is, to select a plan that may be far from optimal but is most likely to "succeed"—with the general obligation to explore all alternatives and select those yielding the optimum results. A timid manager may be tempted to suppress a plan that might fail or else whittle it down to nothing in order not to expose himself to criticism. But that is a bad policy even from the point of view of self-interest. Without a plan, chances are that the firm will not run smoothly and will likely produce results at wide variance with the expectations of senior management. The subordinate-level manager may be exposed to much graver charges than that of having executed plans imperfectly.

Continuity of Tenure

Some time must elapse before a new manager can take sufficient cognizance of a business, the strengths and weaknesses of employees, the resources available, the firm's general setup, and future possibilities, so he can efficiently participate in compiling the plan of action. A manager must also sense a certain permanency in his position rather than feeling his role is only temporary. If he feels that he will not have enough time to complete the plan or only enough to barely begin implementing it, or if he is convinced that his effort is condemned to bear no fruit, or that it will serve only to expose him to criticism, can it be expected that he will carry out his planning duties with enthusiasm or even undertake them unless required to? Human nature must be reckoned with. Without continuity of tenure on the part of management personnel, there can be no good plan of action.

Professional Competence and General Business Knowledge

These abilities are just as necessary for drawing up a plan as for carrying it out. They are pointed out here as a reminder of their importance; further elaboration does not seem necessary.

Planning as a Safeguard Against Incompetence

The foregoing conditions which are essential for compiling a good plan presuppose intelligent and experienced management. By the same token, lack of a plan or a bad plan is a sign of managerial incompetence. To safeguard a business against such incompetence:

1) A plan must be compulsory.

2) Good specimen plans should be made generally available (from past history of the firm, published sources, trade associations, universities, or consultants). Experience and general discussion should help single out those plans to be used as examples.

3) The subject of planning should be covered in the training program for new employees of the organization. It must be given high priority and explained and analyzed for even the lowest ranking employee; planning is a skill which benefits the organization when utilized even in rudimentary form at any level.

4 Organizing

To organize a business is primarily to lay out its human organization—its lines of responsibility and authority, and the expected flow of communications. When equipped with the essential material resources, the body corporate should be capable of fulfilling the six essential management functions and, in the process, carrying out all the activities in which the firm needs to be engaged.

MANAGERIAL DUTIES WITHIN AN ORGANIZATION

Between the body corporate of the one-man business, where a single individual performs all functions, and that of an international concern employing hundreds of thousands of people, there are to be found all possible intermediate stages. In every case, though, the organization should carry out the following managerial duties:

1) Ensure that the plan is judiciously prepared and strictly carried out.

2) See that the human and material organizations are consistent with the objectives, resources, and general operating policies of the concern.

3) Set up a single, competent, energetic guiding authority and establish the lines of communication to and from this authority throughout the organization.

4) Harmonize activities and coordinate efforts.

5) Formulate clear, distinct, precise decisions.

6) Arrange for efficient personnel selection: each department should be headed by a competent, energetic person, and each employee should be in that position where he or she can render greatest service.

7) Define duties clearly.

8) Encourage a liking for initiative and responsibility.

9) Have fair and suitable recompense for services rendered.

10) Make use of sanctions in cases of fault and error.

11) Maintain discipline.

12) Ensure that individual interests are subordinated to the general interest.

13) Pay special attention to unity of command.

14) Supervise both material and human order.
15) Have everything under control.
16) Fight against an excess of regulations, red tape, and paperwork.

The above missions of management can be fulfilled, to a large part, through effective organization of the business. Organizing is simple in the one-man business, but more complex as the enterprise grows larger and its personnel become more numerous. To illustrate this increasing complexity and the role of the body corporate, we will examine some basic principles of organization: 1) Every body corporate shows strong external resemblances to every other one of similar size, although there are differences in the nature and relative value of the constituent elements. 2) The constituent parts of the body corporate may be "organized" into nine levels. 3) Every level of the organization makes specific demands on the individuals at that level; specific abilities and education are needed if the body corporate is to be soundly constructed. 4) Careful selection of business personnel is essential to the strength of the organizational structure established. Training is also a part of organization, but we will leave examination of this aspect of the body corporate to a later chapter.

ORGANIZATION CHARTS

An "organization chart" is a diagram that clearly delineates the structure of authority from higher levels to lower ones and indicates the paths of responsibility, delegation, and communication. Preparation of charts like the simplified ones shown in Figs. 1 and 2 can considerably facilitate the building up and supervising of an organization. Such charts, in contrast to lengthy descriptions, make it possible to quickly grasp the organic whole of an organization, including departments that are in place, the lines of demarcation between functions, and the line of authority. An organization chart can draw attention to weak points, such as overlapping or the encroachment of one department into the domain of another, dual command, and activities that are unstaffed or have no clearly indicated single head. This mode of portraying a firm's organization is suitable for all types of concerns: large establishments as well as small, firms that are either expanding or declining. When used as a tool in a newly formed business, the organization chart is a framework that enables management to indicate various departments that will be present and identify compartments in which employees' names will be written as they are selected. Yet the use of an organization chart is not confined to the period when a business is being formed; scarcely has that task been accomplished when organizational modifications, as a result of changes in circumstances or people, become necessary. Any modification in one part of an organization can have wide repercussions on the general running of the whole. An organization chart offers a particularly good means for anticipating those repercussions and developing ways to head off nega-

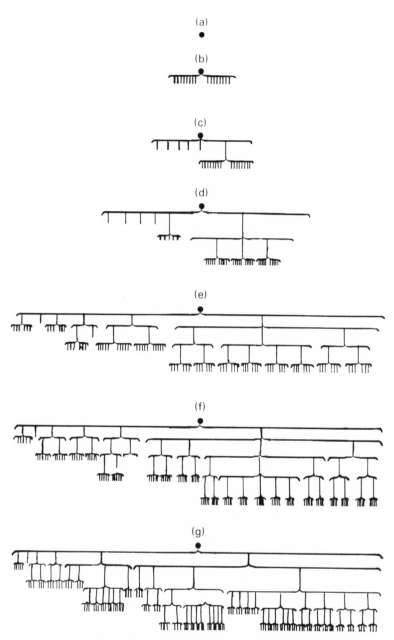

Fig. 1. Form of the organization at various stages of expansion.

tive impacts. To be useful, such a chart must always be kept up to date. Assuming this to be the case, it is a precious managerial instrument.

An organization chart can be used to show each department or function, the person who is in each position, the superior from whom each em-

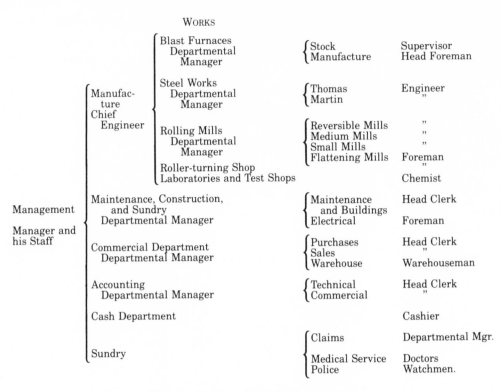

Fig. 2. Organization chart: positions.

ployee takes orders, and the subordinates to whom he gives them. But such a chart cannot generally be used to show the contribution to the firm made by the occupant of the position nor that employee's specific daily activities, the physical limits of the person's responsibility, or who shall assume his duties when that person is absent. Such information belongs on special lists that accompany the organization chart. In industry, various techniques have been developed for presenting these types of information including method charts, procedure charts, personnel utilization charts, job descriptions, and responsibility charts. Whichever method is used, it must be consistent with the main chart, accurate, and kept up to date by regular revisions.

FORM OF THE BODY CORPORATE
AT VARIOUS STAGES OF DEVELOPMENT

The general form of an organization depends on the number of employees, the level and motivation of those employees, and the nature of the work to be done. First, let us consider the stages of growth of an industrial concern and how the organizational structure changes as the number of personnel increases.

1) Stage 1 may be considered that of the solitary craftsman in a one-man business. An organization chart depicting this business has just a single box within which all duties and responsibilities reside. With the box compressed, such an organization is (a) in Fig. 1.

2) Stage 2 is the form taken by the business as the craftsman hires a few workers. They all report directly to the craftsman, and the line of authority goes from him down. As shown by (b) in Fig. 1, a chart of this organization shows lines going down from our previous single box (representing the original craftsman) to each of the other boxes that appear in a row on a second level. We have now introduced a superior/subordinate relationship (between levels one and two).

3) When the number of workers rises to 10, 20, or 30, as the case may be, a foreman (i.e., an intermediary) comes between the head of the enterprise and some of the workers. The organization now has three levels, as shown by (c) in Fig. 1. On the first level, the original craftsman continues to be shown. However, the second level now contains the new foreman and only some of the original second-level workers (with whom the craftsman might wish to retain a direct reporting relationship). The lines of authority run from first level to new foreman and from the first level to each of the workers still on the second level. In addition, new lines of authority stretch from the new foreman to third-level workers, some of whom may be new and some of whom may be former second-level workers "bumped" to the third level.

4) Each new group of 10, 20, or 30 workers brings in a fresh foreman. When there are two, three, or four foremen, a superintendent to oversee the foremen may be necessary as in (d) in Fig. 1. In turn, when there are two or three superintendents, a departmental manager may be needed. The number of links of the scalar chain continues to increase in this way up to the ultimate superior, with each new superior having usually no more than four or five immediate subordinates. On the basis of 15 workers to a foreman or one superior of rank $S(n)$ to every four subordinates of rank $S(n + 1)$, the number of workers in a concern will be as follows:

$S1$	15
$S2$	60
$S3$	240
$S4$	960
$S5$	3840
$S6$	15,360
$S7$	61,440
$S8$	245,760
$S9$	983,040

We quote these figures, those of a simple geometrical progression whose first term is 15 and common ratio 4, to show a structure that lends itself well to the grouping of even large numbers of employees. Furthermore, the number of levels of authority even in the largest of such business concerns is quite small. If each level were to be indicated by a stripe, the number of stripes of the highest industrial leaders would rarely exceed seven; those of the officials of most cities of the world would not exceed eight or nine. The effects of such groupings are to keep the administrative overhead of the organization under tight control and to minimize the number of levels dividing the highest executive officers from those carrying out the physical production of the organization's goods and services. The organization grows to (e), (f), and (g) in Fig. 1.

The motivation and level of the personnel involved also affect the groupings. Where the employees are not motivated to perform a proper day's work, where the nature of the production process is not amenable to ready inspection of the output, or where the output must meet very high quality standards, the closeness of supervision must be increased. One foreman might have to supervise only five or six or even fewer employees. In such instances, the foreman serves as the link between management and worker. His objectives are not only to motivate the workers, but to help make resources available, to keep the workers under control, to keep their activities coordinated—in short, to perform all the managerial functions through constant interaction with the immediate personnel involved. The foreman's communications with those people should be constant, detailed, and amiable to assure that required output and work quality are maintained.

By contrast, in some work locations, the individuals are highly motivated professionals, take a genuine interest in their performance vis-à-vis the quality and integrity of the output, and need very little in the way of direct supervision. Indeed, such personnel are often assigned to duties where they will be remote from their superiors. A large number of such personnel might be under the control of very few administrators. When it is possible to increase the number of workers under the control of any one foreman, it becomes possible, at the same time, to reduce the number of superintendents (two-stripers from our previous analogy), reduce the number of their supervisors (three-stripers, four-stripers, and so on), and thus considerably reduce the number of levels in the organization. The major benefit of such an action, besides reducing administrative costs, is to shorten the chain of communications between the top individual and the production individual. This has enormous repercussions: production workers adapt to new conditions more rapidly, the goals of top management are much more likely to be implemented down to the lowest levels, and performance results at all levels are more accurately transmitted back up to the top for appropriate executive action.

The nature of the work also greatly affects the groupings that are decided on. Essentially, if the worker is tied to or paced by the machine, if the worker's duties lend themselves to ready evaluation of his performance, or if the nature of the payment system is such that the worker has built-in monetary incentives to maintain production, then the supervision can be eased off (although maintenance of quality may become a problem) and larger numbers of workers can be supervised by fewer foremen. In a textile plant where looms are turning out thousands of yards of material, control of the process (aside from loading and unloading the machines) is largely out of the hands of the employee, who only stands by to watch that nothing goes wrong, ties knots into torn threads, and makes minor adjustments to the machines as necessary. The employee's performance is readily checked by examination of the goods coming off the machine. In such a process, a foreman can easily supervise not just 15, but multiples of 15. In shops where garments are sewn by hand and machine, payment systems are such that the worker is directly rewarded for each piece completed; here the foreman need only spot check the quality of the goods being turned out (so that speed is not being gained at the cost of shoddy workmanship), and can keep a count of output as finished goods are turned over to the next processing steps. Again, in such an environment, the ratio of workers to supervisors can be far greater than 15 to 1. The process makes possible a reduction in the number of foremen and superintendents needed; the result is an organization with a much shorter communication path between top executives and production employees. An organization chart showing only the works segment of a firm's structure, and detailing the titles of the personnel who are subordinate to one another, is shown in Fig. 2.

THE SELECTION OF PERSONNEL

Selection, which is the process of obtaining the employees in order to build up an organization and is among the most important and difficult of business activities, exerts considerable influence on an enterprise's eventual fate. The consequences of a bad choice are commensurate with the rank of the employee: a mistake would normally be relatively unimportant in the case of an operative, but is always grave in the case of a higher executive. Difficulty in choosing employees increases with rank; a few days, sometimes a few hours suffice to assess a workman's usefulness, but weeks or months are needed to know the value of a foreman and sometimes years elapse before there can be any exact assessment of the value of the head of a large concern. Hence, it is of utmost importance not to err in the choice of higher managers. It is also crucial to be on guard against a widening and deepening spread of mediocrity in an organization's personnel. A poor top manager wants no "threats" from higher quality subordinates, so he necessarily chooses subordinates "less good" than he. Those people, in turn, want no "threats" from their subordinates, so they select their inferiors. The latter, in turn, will never fill an open position with anyone who appears to have better credentials than they or possesses the intelligence to threaten their jobs. Thus, they too seek their inferiors. This widening spectrum of mediocrity eventually brings disaster to the firm in spite of the seemingly best efforts of all who populate it.

Because such individuals started with limited capacities (indeed, that was why they were chosen), their best efforts will be limited as well.

Large-scale management, especially, presents great difficulties. These difficulties are inherent in the nature of social organizations and have always existed. But what have not always existed are industrial development and the concentration of many industrial units within a given enterprise—trends that have considerably increased the proportion of large-scale concerns. Concentration of industrial units, in which one large-scale enterprise is substituted for a given number of small or medium-sized ones, produces diverse effects. The results are usually similar:

1) Since much larger organic units have been brought into being, men of wider powers are needed than was previously the case in the smaller concerns.

2) At the same time that concentration produces a demand for more capable men, it abolishes a good number of positions that might be regarded as training opportunities for managers.

3) Whereas in a medium-sized concern departmental heads acquaint themselves to some extent with other departments, in a large-scale business each department is sufficiently important to absorb the time and energies of its head. If he is competent, he is likely to attain such a high position in his specialized area that it is the culmination of his career. In such a system, many people with exceptional potential for breaking out of specialty areas, are, nevertheless, excluded from the training ground for general management.

Hence, concentration of industrial units augments the need for higher managers and renders their training more difficult. We could, with profit, devote the rest of this volume to a discussion of this point, but that would stray from our purpose of presenting the broad spectrum of the management process and how to carry it out. However, further in this book, at selected points, we will touch on additional aspects of the development, education, training, and experience of the business employee and provide some advice for those just completing their university work.

FORM OF THE BODY CORPORATE IN DIFFERENT TYPES OF ENTERPRISES

The bodies corporate of enterprises of all kinds are constituted in similar fashion to those of industrial concerns, so much so that all organizations at the same stage of expansion are relatively alike. This likeness occurs because businesses of the same type perform primarily identical functions and because even enterprises of different types have a preponderance of similar functions. There are very close resemblances in businesses of the same kind, and partial but well-marked resemblances in the rest.

The relative emphases placed on different functions will vary. In industrial concerns, technical activities are generally regarded to be of greatest importance; in a commercial concern, commercial activities would be emphasized; in a school, teaching would be stressed, and so on. The most highly developed "organ" of an enterprise is the special function that most directly characterizes it. But, regarded as a whole, the body corporate, given the same stage of development, always retains the same general appearance.

The same general appearance, however, does not imply the same detailed structure or the same organic quality. Of two organizations similar in appearance, one may be excellent and the other bad, depending upon the personal qualities of those individuals who comprise them. If it were possible to ignore the human factor, it would be easy enough to develop an organizational structure that would work every time. Any novice could do it, provided he had some idea of current practices and could count on the necessary funds. But to create a useful organization it is not enough to group people and distribute duties; one must know how to adapt the organic whole to the unique nature of the specific business (its processes, markets), how to find essential personnel, and how to place each individual where he can be of most service. In sum, numerous important qualities are needed in the person who constructs an organizational structure.

The body corporate of a concern is often compared to a machine or plant or animal. The expressions "administrative machine" and "administrative gearing" suggest an organism obeying the drive of its head and having all its effectively interrelated parts move in unison toward the same end. This analogy is excellent, so far as it goes, but it wrongly implies that "administrative gearing" (i.e., every intermediate executive), like mechanical gearing, loses power because it must overcome internal friction and inertia. That is a false concept: the administrative gearing can and must be a *generator* of power and of ideas. Each "gearing" (that is, each intermediary) has a potential power to take the initiative that, when properly used, can add to rather then subtract from higher management's power of action. When the activity of the administrative whole is limited, this is not because power has been dissipated by the inertia or friction of the gearings, but because higher management has not tapped the gearings' potential. And when power at the center is weak, negative forces hold sway.

There have also been numerous comparisons between social units, such as the body corporate, and plant life. A young, single tree trunk develops branches that spread out and grow leaves, and the sap brings life to all branches, even the slenderest twigs, just as higher authority transmits activity right down to the lowest and farthest extremities of the body corporate. Trees "do not grow right up into the sky," and corporate bodies too have their limiting factors. Is the reason insufficient climbing power of the sap in the first instance and insufficient managerial capacity in the second? To continue the analogy, the tree attains a measure of strength through grouping and juxtaposition—namely the forest—that it cannot attain by its isolated growth. Business, for its part, obtains greater strength through agreements, licenses, trusts, and federations. Each industrial unit, keeping a fair measure of autonomy, makes to the common whole a contribution that is largely returned to it. Grouping by juxtaposition is the means whereby powerful associations are formed and whereby strong collective organizations develop with the expenditure of minimum administrative effort.

But it is to the animal sphere that the social organism is most often compared. Man in the body corporate plays a role like that of the cell in the animal—a single cell in the case of the one-man business, a thousandth or millionth part of the body corporate in the large-scale enterprise. As elemental units (men or cells) are grouped together and the organization develops, the limbs appear. In the animal, the limbs take their specific form while other parts of the body are likewise developing and becoming more complex; in the body corporate, the "limbs" of the business—its functions and personnel—are differentiated and perfected as the number of grouped elements increases. In the social organism, as in the animal, a small number of essential functional elements account for an infinite variety of activities. Countless comparisons may be made between the functions of the two kinds of organic units. The nervous system in particular bears close comparison to the managerial information function. Being present and active in every organ, the nervous system normally is not apparent to the superficial observer, but everywhere it receives impressions that it transmits first to the lower centers (reflexes) and thence, if need be, to the brain or organ of direction. From these centers, or from the brain, the order then goes out to the muscles that will be involved in carrying out a given movement. The body corporate, like the animal, has both reflex responses, which take place without immediate intervention on the part of the higher authority, and responses that must pass up to and then down from the brain (the higher authority). Without the activities of the nervous system (or managerial activities), the organism becomes an inert mass and quickly decays.

FUNCTIONING PARTS OF THE BODY CORPORATE

In the one-man business, the entire constituency of the body corporate is just that one person; in a large enterprise, the essential functions become highly complex and involve many people, so numerous differentiated subconstituencies are developed. To study the functioning parts of an undertaking, we will first take as an example a large industrial concern, involved in mining and metallurgy, that is incorporated and employs about 10,000 people. Fig. 3 shows the framework of the company's personnel. Reading from left to right there are first the shareholders, then the board of directors, then general management. Up to that point authority to operate the corporation has been increasingly concentrated at each stage of its transmission. After that it becomes more diffuse via

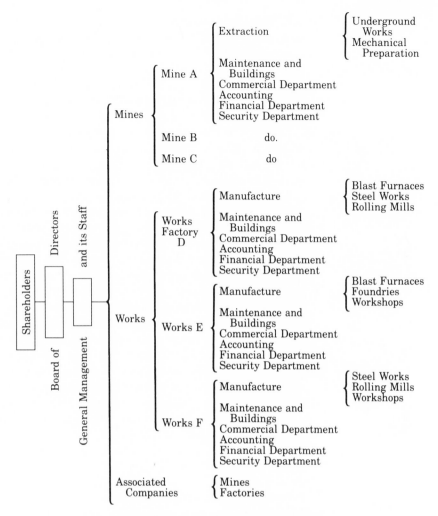

Fig. 3. A large industrial undertaking.

regional and local management and sundry departmental heads. The following members of the body corporate of the company may be identified:

1) Shareholders
2) Board of directors
3) General management and its staff
4) Local management
5) Chief engineers
6) Technical (departmental) managers
7) Superintendents
8) Foremen
9) Operatives

Shareholders

The shareholders' role is very restricted and consists chiefly of 1) appointing members to the board of directors, 2) considering the board's recommendations, and 3) passing on unusual proposals, such as broad pension plans or broad executive compensation plans that go beyond the authority of the board of directors.

The shareholders meet at least once a year, and their most important and most difficult task is the appointment of directors.

The Board of Directors

The powers that the board exercises are granted to it to be used on behalf of the stockholders. The board has wide statutory powers to do such things as declare dividends, effect mergers, and sell assets. Prime responsibilities of the board include, to the maximum extent possible, protecting shareholders' invested capital, ensuring the adequacy of return on that capital, perpetuating the life of the corporation, satisfying the diverse interests of all the shareholders, and reporting to the shareholders. The board of directors appoints members of general management, and delegates to them many of the powers it has in order to ensure the smooth functioning of the corporation. While general management makes most of the decisions, the board of directors exercises control in a general way by monitoring management activities and setting up committees to study specific issues.

General Management

The responsibility of general management is to conduct the enterprise toward its objectives by making optimum use of its resources. It is the executive authority, it draws up the plan of action, selects personnel, sets performance standards, and controls the execution of all activities. There may be one, several, or even more general managers. The solitary general manager may be in direct contact either with local managers or with intermediaries (such as heads of groups of establishments or heads of general, technical, or commercial departments). When there are several general managers, their duties may be assigned by geographical area, by groupings of divisions serving the same markets, or by responsibility for specific projects or problems confronting the firm. But much more important than the system used are the personal qualities of the individuals involved. A group of well-motivated individuals can completely direct and control even the poorest system and force it to produce at a high level, but where there is a lack of this motivation, even the finest system will produce little more than wasted efforts.

In every case, general management should be supported by a staff. The staff is a group of men and women equipped with energy, knowledge, and time that the general manager may lack. The staff, which serves as an adjunct or reinforcement to the manager, might be viewed as an extension of his personality. A large staff structure may have several levels of authority in it, but the staff director reports to, and receives his authority from, the general manager. Such a group is known as "general staff" in the army; this name is used here for lack of any other more preferable.

The general staff is intended to assist the manager in carrying out his personal duties. If it is possible for him to carry out all his obligations unaided, he requires no staff. But if his own energies or knowledge are insufficient, or his time too limited, he is obliged to have help, and it should be provided through the authority to assemble a staff. Few higher level managers are able to deal at one and the same time with the following:

1) Their daily obligations of correspondence, interviews, conferences, and sundry activities.

2) Command and control.

3) Various investigations needed in order to prepare future plans and harmonize current ones.

4) A constant search for improvements that can be introduced into every sphere of activity.

Hence, staffs of various composition are to be found in the majority of large-scale industrial concerns: there are functional specialists (engineering, legal, financial, accounting), consultative committees, research groups, laboratories, and so on. A general staff is particularly necessary if a business needs very specialized assistance to a number of its departments, with the expectation that staff services will cut across departmental lines and across the hierarchy of the organization. Such functions should be lodged in a staff that reports to the general management of the organization.

So that they may be entirely at the general manager's disposal and free of other responsibilities, the members of the staff should not have executive functions in subordinated departments. However, the same person might be attached to the staff for part of his time and to some department for another part of it. A staff need not be exclusively attached to the business. A particular specialist, for instance, may quite usefully give his services to the staff for an hour a day, a day a week, or a day a month. The constitution and functioning of a particular staff lend themselves to a variety of procedures. It is sufficient to say that the staff should be entirely at the general manager's disposal and should, through its assistance, ensure that all the duties of management are performed.

Staff work falls into five categories:

1) Assistance afforded to the manager in dealing with urgent matters, correspondence, interviews, and preparation of records.

2) Liaison and control.

3) Future projects, involving the drawing up of new plans or correcting of existing plans in the light of new information.

4) Performance of organizational development studies.

5) Performance of "completed staff work" (preparation of the research package for the manager's decision/action).

All of the above activities come within the scope of management and, in the interests of the business, have to be done. The manager can attend to them personally, or delegate them to his staff. The first two types of staff work are usually satisfactorily accomplished in any firm worthy of note. But future planning and organizational development—two activities that greatly affect a firm's success—are often deplorably neglected. Often, the duties of a staff are indeed labeled "forward planning," "strategic analysis," or "organization development." Nevertheless, it has not yet become customary to regard the staff function, under managerial impetus, to consist of preparing for the future and to seek out all possible improvements. For the staff to acquit itself satisfactorily of this portion of its role, it must be free of 1) undue influence that causes it to take action against its better judgment, 2) petty considerations, related to internal politics and which lead to poorly conceived actions, and 3) the muting of the staff's voice (as opposed to resolution of differences) when the results of staff analyses contradict the wishes of the hierarchy. The staff should feel no fear of retribution when it "tells the emperor that he, indeed, is wearing no clothes."

In many ways, the staff, more than any other part of the body corporate, makes the greatest demands on management. The manager must pay close attention to the progress of the staff work, bring his judgment and experience to bear on the input he receives, exercise his authority skillfully, and keep a sense of proportion about what the staff tells him. A staff service should be instituted only in the interest of the concern, not for its own sake. It may somewhat take on the appearance of a personal service since it is intended to supplement the necessarily limited capacities of the individual manager. It lends itself easily to abuse and evokes keen critical attention, so in many firms not all of the staff's potential services are utilized.

One of the chief duties of staff is the search for improvements. It is well known that a business which does not go forward is soon behind its competitors, and so progress in every sphere must be pursued unremittingly. To effect improvements, method, ability, time, determination, and financial backing are required. *Method* consists of observing, collecting and filing facts, interpreting them, trying out experiments if need be, and from the study as a whole, deducing rules which, under the management's impetus, may be introduced into business practice. Most developments that have raised business science to its present level emanate from this process. However, it is not sufficient merely to be able to define the method; in order to use it effectively, a manager must have innate abilities developed by experience. He should have a fairly thorough knowledge of the ways in which research can be brought to bear on problems and decisions pertinent to the development of the enterprise. Even the best informed manager cannot be completely competent with regard to all the different kinds of questions arising from an improvement program, any more than he can be familiar with all facets of the management of a vast concern. Managers, absorbed by current work and by weighty questions calling for immediate attention, do not usually have enough time to devote themselves to development research. They must, therefore, allow the staff the freedom and resources to do such work. Once the work has been started, it is sufficient for management to transmit to the staff its determination to keep the business abreast of progress and to monitor the staff's performance in so doing.

The search for improvement should be pursued unceasingly at all levels and throughout all parts of the business. The executive in charge (whether of the whole business, a department, or a workshop) should have an active, unrelenting intention to effect improvements and should be capable of transmitting this intention to his employees. He must act definitively to demonstrate that "sacred cows" or complacency will not be tolerated. In short, he must earn such personal credibility among employees, so that they will cooperate fully as he pursues the necessary investigations. In a large mining and metallurgical concern, for instance, work on improvements is carried out by specialists (metallurgists, mining engineers, civil engineers, architects, electrical engineers, geologists, chemists, lawyers, and accountants) who are grouped around the general manager, some employed full-time and others giving only a part of their time. In local management, the work might be carried out by a staff consisting of technical secretaries, special assistants, research groups, laboratories, and so forth. It is by the close and unbroken collaboration of executives with their staffs that most of the countless improvements filling the pages of technical publications are brought into being.

This emphasis on staff work does not, however, mean that a manager is absolved from making decisions about important technical, commercial, financial, and other matters. In the larger firms—where management actions can have international ramifications, involving large work forces, interactions with complex governmental regulations, and huge sums of money—the top executive will be especially reliant on the advice of department heads and staff. In such complex situations, it is especially important that the staff make sure that "completed staff work" has been performed to the highest professional standards. Completed staff work involves the generation of all the options available for a solution, a decision, or an action (together with supporting data). The staff then suggests one or more options as best, and presents the reasoning for making this choice, while downgrading the others. This mode of operation is used particularly often in the military; the term "completed staff work," in fact, comes from that sphere.

While staff input can be extremely important, the manager should never depend on his staff to cover a lack of competence in the specialized activities that make up the raison d'être of the business; such a practice is inadmissible at any level of the managerial hierarchy. The manager should be thoroughly knowledgeable about the main elements of his enterprise: science and engineering in a technical firm, money in a banking firm, politics in government, war in the military, religion in the church, medicine in the hospital, education in the school, and so on.

In addition, if a manager is responsible for a specific function, he should be thoroughly competent in that function—an accountant must know his accountancy, an attorney must know his law, and so forth. Special demands in terms of competency apply to the type of person chosen to become the chief executive of a firm. As the operating head of the firm, he is charged with seeing to its success in meeting the expectations of the investors. In view of this responsibility, he should not only possess strong general managerial abilities, but should have a special in-depth competency in the function (such as marketing or finance) that the board of directors deems to be presenting the key challenge to the firm.

Local Management

The largest corporations are groupings of entire subsidiary companies; these companies may, in turn, be groupings of massive divisions, and these divisions may, in turn, be groupings of large-scale industrial units. The general management of the corporation represents an extension, carried to its highest level, of the management of the large scale unit which, a case might be made, represents an extension of the smallest units. The principles which govern at any one level do not lose force at any other. An industrial unit might be an agricultural concern, mine, works, or workshop with its headquarters executive personnel. A unit may be small, medium-sized, large, or very large. In a small or medium-sized unit, the local manager is usually in contact with all departmental heads; in a large works, there are frequently one or more levels of management acting as intermediaries between the local manager and the heads of the various functional departments. The local manager's powers depend both on the particular circumstances and on the relative division of powers as between general and local management. Sometimes the local manager's powers verge on autonomy; sometimes they are quite restricted. The personal qualities and knowledge required of the local manager will vary depending on the powers he has been given and the size of the industrial unit for which he is responsible. The head of a large industrial concern, for example, must be primarily a manager rather than a technical specialist. He should have a well-rounded business knowledge with regard to the activities carried out by the firm, the firm's role in the community (especially vis-à-vis governing bodies), and, very importantly, its niche in the marketplace (past, present, and future). While such a person cannot be knowledgeable enough to carry out all the functions personally, he should know what results to expect, know what to do with those results, and, overseeing the various functions, be able to keep the firm operating according to plan. These abilities are the sine qua non of the manager's skills.

Technical (Departmental) Managers, Chief Engineers, Superintendents, Foremen, and Operatives

The general managerial functions, predominant at the top, give place gradually to the more specialized functions—technical, commercial, or other, depending on the firm's main activities—that are the chief preoccupation of those lower in the hierarchy. Such a hierarchy, starting with the chief operating officer, through vice presidents, down to departmental officers, to foremen, then operatives, is to be found, with variations only in format but hardly ever in substance, in enterprises of all kinds: commercial, financial, military, poltical, religious, and other. The management content (as opposed to technical content) and degree of abstraction from the tangible product decrease as one descends the hierarchy. The chief executive deals with earnings, demand, growth, and equivalent sweeping concerns into the distant future. The middle-level manager deals with information on earnings and production in the last quarter and what they are likely to be in the next. The foreman counts his daily production and tries to anticipate problems for the next week at most. The operative is concerned with the tangible work to be done on the next item coming down the assembly line. No level should overlook the concerns and contributions it can make to all the others. While operatives have often been accused of having no interest in the concerns of higher levels, this has probably been due more to lack of opportunity to manifest such concerns than insufficient will or desire. Managers too, often adopt a narrow focus—on the concerns of their level—but this is because of the "conventional wisdom" that as one climbs the hierarchy, the details of a lower level are no longer of importance.

This "wisdom" is over-emphasized by many managers and authors in the management field, and a more balanced view is preferable. While it is true that no one should continue to do the detailed work of the lower positions he leaves behind, a manager is aided in evaluating the work of the lower levels by using knowledge of the details, to probe into what is presented, as part of the review process. It is neglect of the details and restriction in the flow of knowledge from level to level that has broken many an enterprise; managers cannot divorce themselves from the details and must assure that all levels of an organization freely contribute to the others.

Scientific management has been proposed as a methodology for the most efficient operation of the firm from the foreman down. It is the system pioneered by Frederick Winslow Taylor. Taylor's approach differs from the one we have outlined in that he examines the firm from the "bottom up." He starts with the most elemental units of activity—the workers' actions—then studies the effects of their actions on productivity, devises new methods for making them more efficient, and applies what he learns at lower levels of the hierarchy to activities carried out at higher levels in the firm.

Taylor believes in the principle of "functional foremanship." He assigns a staff to help the shop foreman, or any other supervisor, even one who is only at the first level of management; he does not, as is more general practice, follow the rule that staff should exist on the organization chart only among the higher reaches of the managerial structure. If we look specifically at a machine shop, we would see that the staff assigned to a specific foreman would, first, plan that group's work and establish procedures for all tasks that are of a purely clerical nature. Second, the staff would come into direct contact with the workmen by assigning daily work orders, pacing the work, performing repairs, instructing the workmen, and costing and timing the output. Instead of the workers coming into contact with management through the single foreman, they would also be in contact through the several individuals performing the staff functions.

One objective of the system is to relieve the foremen of a number of repetitive functions, giving him more time to oversee production, attend to disruptions in production, and to deal with individual workers who need personal or other help. The foreman must be prepared to answer for any problems with product quality or quantity. Therefore, he is the authority who sets the operating parameters for how the staff is to assist him and his group, serves as liaison with those feeding the work to or receiving work from his group, and ultimately answers to the final user/customer. As Taylor explains it, staff attached to the first level of supervision absolve this individual from having to have special knowledge at his command, relieve him of innumerable interruptions, and allow him to focus more closely on the movement of the product through his operations.

Taylor's recommendations, however, result in a negation of the principle of unity of command. The military type of organization, which has had innumerable successes throughout history and has therefore been copied by so much of industry, calls for one man to lead, give instructions, supervise all the details, and be the center of responsibility for all interactions with the working personnel. Adding a staff to the foreman's management of a department might be reconciled with the principle of unity of command by preventing workers from having direct contact with the staff. The foreman might have an assistant foreman to act as the channel for all communications between workers and staff; the assistant will report directly to the foreman and thus keep him current on all aspects of the work. Where such reconciliation cannot be reasonably well established, with unquestionably "smooth" operations, it is probably best to train the foreman to carry out the work Taylor assigns to the staff and, thereby, maintain the military organization (unity of command).

5 Coordinating

To coordinate is to harmonize all the activities of a concern so as to facilitate its successful functioning. Coordination involves:

1) determining the sequencing and timing of activities so that they properly mesh;
2) allocating to things and actions their rightful proportions of resources, time, and priority;
3) adapting means to ends.

Coordinating involves keeping expenditures, in amount and timing, proportionate to financial resources; equipment and tools proportionate to production needs; stocks proportionate to rate of consumption; and sales proportionate to production. Coordinating means building the house neither too small nor too big, adapting the tool to its use, the road to the vehicle, the safety precautions to the risks. It means keeping the secondary considerations behind the principal ones. It involves, in a word, bearing in mind the consequences of any activity—technical, commercial, financial, or other—on all the other functions of the business.

In a well-coordinated enterprise, the following situations prevail:

1) Each department works in harmony with the rest. The warehouse knows what has to be supplied and at what time; production knows its target; maintenance keeps equipment and tools in good order; finance procures necessary funds; security sees to the protection of goods and personnel—and all these activities are carried out in a properly paced, orderly fashion.
2) In each department, divisions and subdivisions are precisely informed as to the share they must take in the communal task and the reciprocal aid they are to give one another.
3) The working schedules of the various departments and their subdivisions are constantly attuned to circumstances.

For such results to be achieved, intelligent, experienced, active direction is needed. The above three requirements are not always fulfilled; in some concerns, the following signs of unmistakable lack of coordination are apparent:

1) Each department knows and wants to know nothing about the others. It operates as if it were its own aim and end, without bothering about either neighboring departments or the business as a whole.

2) The divisions and offices of the same department, as well as different departments, operate in a narrowly compartmentalized way. Each one's prime concern is to take cover from personal responsibility behind a piece of paper, an order, or a circular letter. (Memos substitute for actions; where there are no actions, there are no mistakes; where there are no mistakes, there is no blame.)

3) No one thinks of the general interest; initiative and loyalty are nonexistent.

This attitude on the part of the personnel, so disastrous for the concern, is not the result of preconcerted intention, but rather it is the culmination of nonexistent or inadequate coordination. A good staff will quickly weaken if it is not constantly reminded of its duties toward the firm and toward all members of the body corporate. One of the best methods for keeping the personnel functioning well and for making the execution of their duties easier is a conference of departmental heads.

The objectives of a conference of departmental heads are to inform management about the running of the concern, to clarify the types of cooperation expected between various departments, and to utilize the presence of departmental managers for solving various problems of common interest. Such conferences do not involve drawing up the plan of action of the business, but rather facilitating the carrying out of this plan in the light of current events. Each conference covers only a short period—normally the coming week—during which the activities are to be harmonized and efforts focused in the manner discussed during the conference.

Here, by way of example, is the practice followed, with excellent results, by the various mines and works of a large mining and metallurgical enterprise. In each mine or works, all departmental heads meet once a week, on a specified day, under the chairmanship of the general manager. Each departmental head indicates how his department is running, difficulties met with, help needed, and solutions suggested. The general manager invites everyone's opinions on all questions which arise or which he himself brings up, and, after discussion, decisions are made. To ensure that no point is omitted from the agenda, minutes are kept of each meeting and read out at the beginning of the following one; these are usually kept by a secretary, who is not one of the departmental managers. The meeting always takes place on its appointed day, even if the general manager cannot be present. In that case, he is represented by a deputy appointed beforehand: one who has an in-depth knowledge of the general manager's viewpoint and is empowered to act completely in his stead at the meeting.

The conference brings together heads of production, extraction, selling, maintenance, buildings, and so forth, and thanks to the pooling of abilities and diversity of viewpoints, the general manager can examine each point with a breadth, precision, and speed otherwise unobtainable. In a relatively short time—about an hour—the general manager is informed about how things are generally going, can make decisions touching various departments simultaneously, can obtain feedback, and can explicitly prescribe how different departments are to help one another. Each departmental head goes away knowing exactly what he has to do, anticipating that he is to return in a week's time to give an account of what he has accomplished. Such cohesion, face-to-face discussion, and attendant commitment could not be obtained without a conference even if ten times more time and effort were to be expended.

Therefore, the general manager should take great care of this precious instrument and prepare for the conference by noting beforehand the matters to be dealt with and supervising the drawing up of the minutes. He should seek to keep the discussion always on courteous terms, and ensure that the agenda is followed in a way that is efficient and of interest to all. The general manager, and his deputy, must be equipped through natural gifts, experience, or training to run a well-managed meeting of this type; otherwise it may be fruitless and boring. Other things being equal, the general manager who is capable of making good use of conferences is much superior to the one who cannot do so.

Experience has shown that a coordinating conference once a week is enough for most types of establishments, whether they have several hundred or thousands of employees. A weekly meeting of departmental heads is indispensable for purposes of coordination in the case of very large units and government agencies; it should be a binding obligation, as well, for other concerns of all sizes and types.

For the conference to be held properly, all departmental heads should be assembled, despite distance barriers or other problems. In the case of exceptional difficulties, the meetings may, on occasion, be held at longer intervals, but if it is impossible for a departmental head to attend any meeting, the gap must be filled by the use of a liaison officer at the meeting. Too often, the general manager himself takes on the liaison officer role, believing that he knows a particular operation in his chain of command so deeply and comprehensively that he can stand in for the missing head with little loss to the discussions that take place. Such an attitude is a mistake. Because of the broad span of his responsibilities, the general manager is unlikely to have the in-depth specialized knowledge of subordinates who are actually doing the jobs. The absent departmental head should choose as a liaison officer an employee who, depending on the circumstances, either has special abilities or is particularly well versed in the questions to be discussed at the meeting. A liaison officer is specially charged with representing his department in the place of the head who cannot attend. Rather than sitting as a mere substitute observer, he should be able to commit the department to a course of action to the same degree as the missing departmental head. All decisions made while he is present should be as binding upon the department as if the head himself had made those commitments.

While coordination is needed in a small establishment, it is a great deal more important in a large-scale concern comprising several separate establishments remote from one another. Combined action is needed on the part of general management, which supervises the whole, and local managements, whose efforts are directed toward the successful working of each particular part. To establish harmony among the various parts of a large concern—that is, among its technical, commercial, financial, and other activities—not only are a good plan and a good organization required, but also continuous coordination. All the forces in play must be kept in equilibrium, and management should not allow a department to take a narrowly conceived action that might create a sudden disturbance threatening the running of the whole. No procedure is better than the conference for ensuring unity of direction, for focusing efforts, and for producing spontaneous collaboration on the part of different departmental heads called upon to pursue a common aim. The problem of narrow compartmentalization disappears when all departmental heads have to give an account of themselves and be in agreement in the presence of a higher authority.

The coordinating conference is to coordination what the plan of action is to foresight and what summarized charts of personnel are to the human organization: it is an essential instrument and a characteristic sign of commitment to a basic managerial function. If the sign is missing, there is a good chance that the function is being badly carried out. On the other hand, the presence of such a sign—the holding of weekly conferences—is no absolute guarantee of smooth working, and, in addition, the manager must know how to use the instrument properly. The art of manipulating this instrument and others is one of the basic qualities required of the manager.

6 Commanding

An organization, having been formed, must be set going—and this is the mission of command. The mission is spread over the different heads of the concern, each in charge of and responsible for his particular unit. For every manager, the objective of command is to get the optimum return from all employees in the unit while, at the same time, furthering the interests of the whole concern.

The art of command rests on certain personal qualities and on a knowledge of general principles of management. It shows up in both small and large concerns, and like all other arts it has its degrees of proficiency. Any sort of very large unit that functions properly and yields a maximum return or benefit inspires public admiration. In every sphere—industrial, military, political, or other—command of a large unit calls for exceptional qualities. While the qualities needed are highly complex, we will confine ourselves here to setting forth a few of the main precepts that facilitate command. The manager who has to command should:

1) Gain a thorough knowledge of his personnel.
2) Eliminate the incompetent.
3) Be well versed in the agreements binding the business and its employees.
4) Set a good example.
5) Conduct periodic audits of the organization using summary charts as needed.
6) Bring together his chief assistants by means of conferences at which he provides for unity of direction and ensures that efforts are focused.
7) Not become engrossed in detail.
8) Aim at making unity, energy, initiative, and loyalty prevail among the personnel.

GAIN A THOROUGH KNOWLEDGE OF THE PERSONNEL

Faced with a unit numbering hundreds or thousands of workers, the high-level manager may at first sight think it impossible to gain a thorough knowledge of his personnel. However, the structure of the organization makes it possible to effect a compromise. Whatever his level of authority, one manager usually has direct command over a small number of subordinates, normally fewer than six. Only the superior S1 (foreman or his equivalent) is in direct command of 20 or 30 employees, when the work is simple. So it is possible for the manager, even in a large-scale concern, to make a study of his immediate subordinates and succeed in knowing what he can expect of each of them and what degree of confidence he can place in them. This study always demands some time and is increasingly difficult as the subordinates go higher in rank; their functions separate them from one another, and contacts between superiors and subordinates become less frequent. Another factor that can make such study difficult is instability of tenure among higher personnel. Retirements, promotions, demotions, and departures keep executive ranks in a constant flux; getting to know their occupants under the dynamic conditions of a business even over the long term is difficult. As for indirect subordinates—that is, those who level by level extend down from the apex of the pyramid (the manager) to its base and who interact primarily with intermediaries—the manager will obviously have less knowledge of them as their number increases. He can still observe and speak with such subordinates, but the duration and frequency of these interactions will necessarily be limited.

ELIMINATE THE INCOMPETENT

To keep his unit in good running order, the manager must separate or suggest separation of any employee who, for whatever reason, has become incapable of carrying out his duties. This essential part of the manager's job is always onerous and often thorny. A decision to separate an employee should be the culmination of careful thought, not an impetuous whim. The employee must have been fairly and equitably assigned work that he was capable of performing or capable of being trained to do. The employee's performance must have been fairly and objectively appraised and honest feedback given to him. The employee must have been given every opportunity to obtain additional training if that could have overcome the poor performance; he must have been given guidance and, where possible, reassigned to other work and given a chance to show proper performance there. At all stages, when his performance failed to improve, he should have been given written warnings of all impending corrective or disciplinary measures. Above all else, management must be sure that procedures have been followed to protect the employee against bias and inequities throughout the entire appraisal process.

Despite all such efforts there will be times when separation is the most reasonable alternative. Consider, for instance, the case of an executive in a high position, well liked by all his colleagues, who has given conscientious service to the company but whose faculties, without his realizing it, are waning to the point of impeding the working of the business. If there is no company policy covering the situation, the executive's superior will be solely responsible for judging whether separation is necessary and determining the precise moment for action. This manager, recalling the services that the man has rendered, feeling personal affection for him, and dreading the inevitable repercussions of a separation, may be inclined to postpone a step that will surprise and deeply distress a respected and loyal employee. However, the common good of the enterprise, of which the manager is judge and steward, requires that the separation be made without delay. The manager must keep in mind that that is his duty and carry it out as courageously as possible.

The manager is correct to anticipate repercussions. The entire body corporate will feel the effect of the amputation of one of its members—an important member at that—and the individual employees will find their senses of security disturbed as well. Their confidence in the future, and consequently their morale and productivity, will be lessened unless they are convinced that the separation was a just and necessary action, carried out as part of an equitable, objective process in the most humane manner possible. Part of the manager's job is to convey to employees that this was the case.

In a concern that has made provisions against the eventuality of such terminations, the superior will have some options in dealing with the employee. Special compensation or nonfinancial rewards may be proffered, or the employee may be asked to reduce his activities to part-time and taper off to fewer and fewer hours. The able and humane manager finds in such expedients and in his own feelings the means for salving wounds that are being inflicted (including wounds to the employee's pride) and at the same time finds ways of reassuring all members of the staff about their futures.

KNOWLEDGE OF AGREEMENTS BINDING THE BUSINESS AND ITS EMPLOYEES

An enterprise and its employees are bound together by agreements, written and unwritten, spoken and unspoken, that arise from the culture in which the firm operates, from law and other professions, from the mores of the workplace, and from the best of past practices. The manager must see that such agreements are carried out. This imposes a dual role on him; he must defend the interests of the business when employees are taking unfair advantage, and defend the interests of employees when the employer is taking unfair advantage. All sorts of human tendencies and failings may come into play. Operatives may want more pay for less work; employees at any level may take actions that stem from laziness, vanity, or other human weakness. It is especially reprehensible when the head of the firm forgets that the interests of the concern as a whole should be the sole criterion of his conduct. He should studiously avoid anything savoring of favoritism involving family, fellow workers, or friends.

To fulfill his role of protecting the firm's interests, the manager should have integrity, tact, and drive. To protect the personnel against possible abuses on the employer's part, he should have full knowledge of the pertinent agreements and strong senses of duty and equity. The mere fact that he adheres to agreements does not free him from obligations of conscience, if an agreement, for example, permits a firm to exploit an employee unfairly. The existence of the agreement does not absolve the manager of all responsibility.

Agreements, be they good or bad, do not last forever; there always comes a time when they are no longer attuned to current economic or social conditions. Periodic changes in agreements are needed, or else there is a risk that someday a formidable conflict will arise. No one is better placed than the manager of his unit for adhering to agreements and for recommending and carrying out, if he has the power, modifications made necessary by changing times and circumstances.

SET A GOOD EXAMPLE

It is taken for granted that managers can exact some measure of obedience through fear of discharge. There are other ways of achieving discipline that draw more on the spontaneous efforts and initiative of workers. Some leaders get obedience, energy, zeal, and loyalty without apparent effort; others never succeed in evoking these qualities.

One of the most effective methods of motivating employees is by example. When the manager sets an example of punctuality, no one else dares to arrive late; when he is active, courageous, and loyal, he is imitated; and, if he knows his job, his subordinates will find their own work more enjoyable. But bad example, too, is contagious, and in coming from above it has very serious repercussions on the unit as a whole. That is one of the countless reasons why a manager must be productive and effective; not only his work, but the work of others is at stake.

AUDIT THE ORGANIZATION PERIODICALLY

It would be most improvident to fail to make periodic inspections of all parts of a machine, especially a complex one. There would be risk of poor output, accidents, even catastrophes. Occasional, superficial inspections would be no adequate guarantee that the machine was in good working order. And regular inspections would be needed to indicate when a complete overhaul was needed.

No less great is the need for periodic overhaul of the administrative machinery, but it is much less widely practiced. One reason for this is that there are few clear guidelines for the form an organization should take. While it is possible to clearly establish what a machine part should be like when in proper running order, there are seldom very precise ideas as to how the more organic aspects of an organization (managers and their subordinates) should operate. The choice of appropriate organizational structure, out of the various forms available, is very difficult; if the existing structure is to be retained, the type of repair work needed on it does not very often appear with clarity. Correction of personnel-related matters usually demands more time, skill, and courage than does correction of the manner in which a concrete task is performed. In matters of personnel, a sense of high moral responsibility must be at the foundation of reform. So it is wise to have a rule that automatically requires periodic inspection of the organization to see whether an overhaul is needed.

It is recommended that every year, in connection with the drawing up of the annual plan, a scrupulous study of the structure of the organization be made with the assistance of summarized charts. These charts should indicate the scalar chain of the organization's managerial staff including the titles of the immediate superior and subordinate of every person; the charts are a kind of photograph of the framework of the concern at a given moment. Charts made up at different dates will show modifications in the composition of the organization that have taken place in the interim. They are invaluable for periodic audits, and no less so for current use, in order to identify any faulty arrangements that may have resulted from hasty modifications in personnel structure. Such flaws in structure, difficult to appreciate from oral or written description, leap into view on a chart. For example, a chart may reveal an indirect command structure in which one superior determines the manner in which work is to be done, or results achieved, while another superior is responsible for overall supervision of the individual, performance appraisal, and decisions about promotion or termination. Such a form of organization leads to dual command, which is the source of many conflicts.

Highly professional employees who can subordinate all other considerations to the performance of their technical work may not have difficulty with a structure burdened by indirect command complications. They focus on the technical aspects of their work, care little for administrative niceties, and interact only with the supervisor of the technical area; this, effectively, restores a form of unity of command and minimizes the destructive effects of the indirect complication. But other employees, those who are not so secure in their positions, will function well only if the two supervisors cooperate very closely to make sure the employees experience no conflicts concerning the type and quality of work they should be doing. In any indirect command structure, there is potential for continuing underlying conflict with attendant costs to the firm. Summarized charts, which give personnel assignments and duties, the structure and lines of authority, and the allocation of responsibilities, reveal the nature of any conflicts that exist and the splits in responsibilities that must be dealt with. Thus, they can help superiors to resolve matters that confuse employees or interfere with productivity.

ARRANGE FOR CONFERENCES AND REPORTS

In a conference attended by his staff and assistants, the manager may explain a program, solicit each person's ideas, make decisions, make sure that his orders are understood, and ascertain that each person knows the part he is to play in the implementation of any decisions made. Such conferences, when they are well planned and carefully controlled, can accomplish all this in a tenth of the time that it would have taken the manager to arrive at the same result otherwise. The personal contact provided by conferences is especially valuable when the assistants in question are important departmental heads. Without frequent contact between them and their chief, verbal as well as crucial nonverbal messages are lost, especially in a very large business. Conferences are a key component of command; the time and trouble that they entail are worthwhile in view of the myriad benefits that face-to-face meetings can yield.

Reports are also important tools. It is the manager's responsibility to know all that goes on, either through personal contact, as in the case of the small unit, or indirectly, as in the large one. Oral and written reports are needed in order to ensure proper supervision and control.

DO NOT BECOME ENGROSSED IN DETAIL

A serious weakness found in some higher managers is a tendency to devote much time to details that subordinates could attend to as well as, or perhaps better than, the manager, with the result that there is no time available to solve important problems. Some people think they are very useful if they deal with the most minute details in person. They cannot get used to the idea that a thing can be done well even if they have not had a hand in it; this way of thinking leads some of them to leave matters in abeyance, deferring action, whenever they cannot be actively involved in a given matter. A higher manager should always seek to reserve for himself enough time to think through the main issues facing the business and to exercise overall direction and control. He should delegate to his subordinates and general staff all the work that he himself is not strictly bound to perform in order to ensure that he will have sufficient time and energy left to address the more important matters claiming his personal attention. Not being engrossed in detail does not mean that details can be disregarded, as discussed in an earlier chapter of this book. A manager should be aware of everything, but he cannot do everything; the care lavished on small matters should not result in his neglecting the large ones. A good organizational structure can help ensure that this does not occur.

MAKE UNITY, ENERGY, INITIATIVE, AND LOYALTY PREVAIL

The manager can make a great contribution toward unity of personnel by brushing aside the seeds of dissension that might be engendered by dual command, ill-defined functions, unmerited reproofs, and so on. He can develop initiative among his subordinates by allowing them the maximum amount of responsibility consistent with their positions and capabilities, even at the cost of some mistakes. The magnitude of the mistakes can be minimized by watchful attention. By discreetly showing employees instead of acting for them, by encouraging them with appropriate praise, by sometimes sacrificing his own personal vanity for their benefit, he can quickly transform people with latent abilities into employees of the first rank. Furthermore, by seeing that this approach is taken at all levels of authority, he can improve the productivity of the work force as a whole.

In contrast, initiative and loyalty will be quickly dried up if the manager is aloof and half-attentive, and he rejects or indefinitely postpones every proposal put forward by his subordinates. The attitudes of personnel can be quickly changed, either for good or for ill, by able or misguided management.

Many other items of advice might be singled out as facilitating the manager's task of commanding his employees. Experience has shown that there are many instruments at the manager's disposal. But it must be remembered that even the best instrument will depend, for its final output, on the skill of the player who uses it.

7 Controlling

Control consists of verifying whether everything occurs in conformity with the plan adopted, the instructions issued, and the principles established, and then taking the appropriate corrective actions. Control involves monitoring for weaknesses, errors, and drifts from the assigned path, rectifying these discrepancies, and preventing their recurrence. Control touches on everything: things, people, actions, timing. In order for the control function to be operative, management must ensure that 1) a plan does exist; 2) the plan is put into operation and kept up to date; 3) the organization of personnel has been completed and summarized personnel charts are in use; 4) command is being exercised in line with principles; 5) coordinating conferences are being held; and 6) corrective machinery has effectively been activated to ensure that the (original) desired results are attained.

From the commercial standpoint, management must make sure that incoming and outgoing materials are checked for quantity, quality, and price—that both the supply and marketing sides of operations are being properly and imaginatively carried out.

From the technical standpoint, management must monitor the progress of operations (both results and any deficiencies that are identified), the development of new products and processes and the improvement of old ones, the maintenance and conditions of plants, and the workings of men and machines.

From the financial standpoint, control must be exercised with regard to financial resources and requirements, capital, and operating budgets. Financial executives must manage the firm's liquid assets, establish the most advantageous tax structure, and provide the capital for ensuring growth. All of these facets are carefully monitored up and down the hierarchy of the line of command, through the finance department itself, and through the operations of committees and task forces.

From the accounting function come the essential documents giving the picture of the condition of the business: reports, statistics, and diagrams that permit management to audit every function. Furthermore, accounting generates the crucial liquidity and other ratios that management uses in comparing operations of the firm against standards that have been set or against competitors' operations, or in determining alternative uses for the funds presently invested in operations.

Finally, security procedures assure that the firm's mental and physical assets are being protected so that risks are eliminated, minimized, or at least brought to management's attention. The potentially hazardous effects of risks that remain are ameliorated by duplication (providing backups to key installations), redundancy (building spare capacity), and insurance.

Normally, these operations are carried out by line employees, with directives for control stemming from the head of the business down through his assistants along the scalar chain. Each department supervises its own employees while higher management keeps an eye on everything. But when certain control operations become too numerous, complex, or widespread to be carried out by ordinary employees of various departments, recourse must be made to special people called controllers (or inspectors).

We focus here on control (as opposed to inspection, which is usually concerned with technical operations and may be considered a subpart of control). The controller is concerned with general management, whose objective is to see that results match the established plans and whose activities are designed to contribute to the smooth working of each department, in particular, and of the concern, in general. For control to be effective, monitoring must be constant, be followed up by corrective actions, and, where appropriate, must carry sanctions. Obviously, if the conclusions derived from checking activities, however efficient, come to hand too late to be of possible usefulness, then control will have been a futile activity. Just as clearly, control is useless if the practical outcomes of it (corrections and sanctions) are neglected. Good management does not allow these two mistakes to be made.

A further danger to avoid is too much infiltration of the control function into management and departmental operations. Such encroachment makes for duality of management, with all the accompanying formidable problems. It can do widespread harm, frequently leaving the operating department with a "checking and correcting" as opposed to a "making and selling" organization, which is often a hostile dichotomy. The tendency on the part of control to encroach is fairly common in large-scale operations especially and may have very serious consequences. To avoid such encroachments, the powers of the controller must be defined at the outset as precisely as possible, with an indication of limits that are not to be exceeded, and then higher management must carefully watch the use that control makes of its powers.

The inspection function usually has a narrower range of duties than that of control. Most inspectors involve themselves with the production process to ensure that the products of the firm match their specifications. They may also be charged with ensuring that the specifications have been correctly drawn. A good inspector must be both competent and impartial. Clearly, the inspector must be competent if he is to be judge of the quality of a product, the value of a manufacturing process, the clarity of the written word, or the interpretation of a complex specification. Impartiality rests on an upright conscience and on the complete independence of the inspector vis-à-vis the person or thing being inspected. More specifically, the following applies:

1) The inspection organization should be isolated from the producing parts of the organization. The work of the inspection department should not be influenced by the department charged with achieving production targets.

2) The inspectors should be isolated from the workers being inspected organizationally, professionally, and even socially. Where the consequences of even the mildest form of collusion are unacceptable, the company must go out of its way to actively discourage any form of in- or out-of-plant social interactions. Control is suspect when the inspector is in any way dependent on the person under inspection or even when the two are linked too closely by similarities of off-duty interests, family relationships, or friendship.

While the inspector should have the qualities of competence, judgment, and tact, it is perhaps most important that he have a sense of duty independent of the persons and chain of command being inspected.

Management is ultimately responsible for determining whether or not control is functioning effectively. Properly carried out, control is a precious auxiliary to management and can provide it with certain necessary data that official supervision might at times fail to furnish. Control can operate on all facets of the business. A good system of control helps prevent undesirable surprises; it provides for turning the "lemon" into lemonade. Control activities provide an opportunity for people to take the initiative in planning against deviations, to head off forces that might cause a deviation, to make corrections very quickly when a deviation does occur, and finally, to redirect the firm to capitalize on a deviation when correction is less feasible. The control function, in that it is applied to all kinds of activities and employees of all grades, operates in a thousand different ways. Like the other elements of management—planning, organization, coordination, and command—control demands constant and sustained attention and often a good deal of art.

8 General Principles of Managing the Body Corporate

The managerial function is exercised through the members of the organization, that is, through the body corporate. While accounting, security, and other functions bring into play money, material, and machines, the managerial function operates mainly through personnel. The soundness and good working order of the body corporate depend on a certain number of conditions that might be termed principles, laws, or rules. Here, we will adopt the term "principles," although this term should be dissociated from any suggestion of rigidity, for there should be nothing rigid or absolute in management affairs. Adhering to a principle is simply a question of proportion. Seldom is the same principle applied twice under identical conditions; allowance must be made for different circumstances and for highly variable elements in the total organizational picture.

Principles that are established should be viewed as flexible, capable of adaptation to every need. It is the manager's job to know how to make use of them, which is a difficult art requiring intelligence, experience, decisiveness, and, most important, a sense of proportion. Compounded of tact and experience, a sense of proportion is one of the key attributes of a manager; this sense determines which of the infinite number of principles of management are to be applied to any situation and to what degree. Why an infinite number? Because there is no limit: every rule or managerial procedure that strengthens the body corporate, or facilitates its functioning, has a place among the principles, at least as long as experience confirms its worthiness. Any change in the firm's internal or external state of affairs can be cause for altering the rules.

The principles of management guide the process of management (planning, organizing, and so forth). Following are 14 principles that have been found to be universally applicable and of particular worth as guiding philosophies in carrying out the process of management.

1) Division of work
2) Authority and responsibility
3) Discipline
4) Unity of command
5) Unity of direction

6) Subordination of the individual's interests to the general interest
7) Remuneration of personnel
8) Centralization
9) Scalar chain (line of authority)
10) Order
11) Equity
12) Stability of tenure of personnel
13) Initiative
14) Esprit de corps

DIVISION OF WORK

Specialization belongs to the natural order; it is observable in the animal world, where the more highly developed the creature the more highly differentiated its organs; it is observable in human societies, where the more important the body corporate the closer is the relationship between structure and function. For example, a family organization may have a loose structure with no formally appointed officers—everyone does what is perceived to be necessary to keep the group functioning. However, should that same organization take on the responsibility for a sick family member, the group will have to open a bank account, appoint responsible family members who will act as de facto officers (treasurer, chairman, secretary, at least), and plan regular meetings. The structure has grown to cope with its new function. In a similar manner, as a society grows, so do new organs develop to replace the single one performing all functions in the more primitive state.

The objective of division of work is to produce more and better work with the same effort. The worker who always makes the same part, or the manager who is always concerned with the same matters, acquires an ability, sureness, and accuracy which, with the caveats mentioned below, usually lead to increased output. Each change of work brings in its train an adaptation that reduces output. Division of work permits a reduction in the number of items to which attention and effort must be directed and has been recognized as a means of making best use of individuals and groups of people in cases where large numbers of identical products must be produced.

Division of work is not restricted to mass production, but is applicable to a wide variety of tasks in which a considerable number of people, varied abilities, or varied machinery is involved. It results in specialization of functions and separation of powers, phenomena that are especially important 1) when information must be kept secret and the "need to know" restricted, 2) when tight control must be maintained over a resource such as money, and 3) when the extreme complexity of a process demands close attention to all details.

Although its advantages are widely recognized, division of work has limits that experience and a sense of proportion teach us should not be exceeded. Division of labor creates boredom, and since a worker may have difficulty focusing continuously on a narrow task, quality can become a serious problem. Furthermore, the loss of worker interest in the job can kill initiative, willingness to change, and ability to meet production quotas. Where the job allows, management must fit the degree to which the job is divided to the interests and abilities of the workers. The workers might be challenged by more duties over a longer cycle of time (job enlargement: horizontal growth) or by more complex and responsible segments (job enrichment: vertical growth).

AUTHORITY AND RESPONSIBILITY

Authority is the right to give orders and the power to exact obedience. A distinction must be made between a manager's official authority, derived from the position he holds, and his personal authority, compounded of intelligence, experience, technical knowledge, moral worth, ability to lead, past services, and so on. In the makeup of a good manager, personal authority is the indispensable complement of official authority. Authority should not be conceived of apart from responsibility, that is, apart from the rewards or penalties that go with the exercise of power. Responsibility is the corollary of authority, its natural consequence and essential counterpart, and wherever authority is exercised, responsibility is also present.

The need for rewards or penalties is part of our sense of fair play or justice; in the general interest, useful actions have to be encouraged and their opposite discouraged. One role of higher management is to apply sanctions to managers who have exercised their authority with poor results, or provide rewards when results have been good. It is not easy to carry out this role, especially in large concerns. It is necessary to establish the manager's responsibility for a specific act or event, determine the exact role played by that individual vis-à-vis the roles of those who have joint or partial responsibility, and then decide on what degree of punishment or reward is appropriate.

The difficulty of assessing responsibility varies with the level in the hierarchy. It is relatively easy to establish a workman's responsibility for his acts and to develop a scale of corresponding sanctions; in the case of a foreman it is more difficult. Proportionately, as one goes up the scalar chain of a business, as work grows more complex, as the number of workers involved increases, and as the final result becomes more remote, it is increasingly difficult to isolate the contribution of the initial act of authority to the ultimate result and to establish the degree of responsibility of the manager. Attempts to measure individual responsibility (or the tangible results flowing from it) have resulted in a number of systems such as responsibility charting, management by objectives, and work incentive programs. Each system has its supporters and detractors, and thousands of words have been written about them and others, but the definitive system remains to be developed.

In developing a reward or penalty system, management must concern itself with what kinds of actions are to be covered, what rewards or punishments are customary, and what timing is to be used; responsibility should be assessed as accurately and equitably as possible. In judging an individual, one must take into account the action itself, the attendant circumstances, and potential repercussions. A manager who makes these types of judgments should have high moral character, impartiality, and firmness. If all of these conditions are not fulfilled, there is a danger that a sense of responsibility may disappear from the concern.

A willingness to accept and valiantly bear responsibility is a kind of courage that is much appreciated nearly everywhere. Tangible proof of this is found in the salary levels of some organization leaders, which are much higher than those of staff personnel who have comparable rank but carry no responsibility. Nevertheless, people who gladly accept responsibility are not the norm. Generally speaking, responsibility is feared as much as authority is sought after, and fear of responsibility paralyzes much initiative and destroys many good qualities. A good leader should possess and infuse into those around him courage to accept responsibility, while the organization sets up safeguards against the inappropriate assumption of authority.

There are two main safeguards against abuse of authority. The first is personal integrity and high moral character; management must demand ethical behavior on the part of all employees so that a climate of integrity becomes the norm. The second safeguard is an ingrained goal orientation that is congruent with the orientation of the governing body of the organization. This involves knowledge of where the business is attempting to go, why it is attempting to get there, and the modus operandi by which it will arrive there. The resulting senses of direction and growth, even excitement, become a part of the individuals serving the firm; management does not have to fear the abuse of a position from one who has internalized what is expected in the way of performance and results. These two senses, of integrity and goal orientation, are conferred neither by election nor by ownership of a share of the business. They come from within the individual as a result of a way of life that embraces those principles; they arise from parents, the social environment, the profession, and, most importantly, from the organization itself.

DISCIPLINE

Discipline is in essence obedience, application, energy, behavior, and outward marks of respect observed in accordance with the standing agreements between the firm and its employees. Whether they have been freely debated or accepted without prior discussion, whether they be written or implicit, whether they derive from the wishes of the parties to them or from rules and customs, it is these agreements which determine the formalities of discipline.

Discipline, being the outcome of a variety of agreements, naturally appears in diverse forms: obedience, application, energy, outward marks of respect, and so on. Forms of discipline vary from one firm to another, from one group of employees to another, and from one time to another. Nevertheless, general opinion strongly holds that discipline is absolutely essential for the smooth running of a business and that without discipline no enterprise can prosper.

This sentiment is very forcibly expressed in military handbooks, where it is often stated that "discipline constitutes the chief strength of armies." This aphorism could be accepted unreservedly were it followed by this one: "Discipline is what leaders make it." The first statement inspires respect for discipline, which is a good thing, but it tends to eclipse from view the responsibility of leaders for establishing that discipline. When a defect in discipline is apparent, or when relations between superiors and subordinates leave much to be desired, responsibility for this breakdown should not automatically be cast on the poor state of "the team." Usually, the problem is primarily a result of the ineptitude of the leaders. It should be emphasized that the state of discipline of any group of people essentially depends on the worthiness of its leaders.

The agreements upon which discipline is based should be as well defined as the command structure. It is important that they be clear and, so far as possible, afford satisfaction to both sides. This is not easy. Proof of that is provided by those strikes which jeopardize the life of a company and greatly inconvenience the public and which arise out of dispute over agreements or out of total failure to even fashion an agreement. The nature of the agreements between a concern and its employees has changed greatly in the last half-century. The agreements of former days, fixed by the employer alone, have been replaced by agreements shaped by general industry practices and by understandings arrived at variously through discussion between management and workers' associations, between management and key employees (whose individual agreements become the model for others), and between management and the individuals comprising the body of the work force. Thus, each executive's responsibility for personnel matters has been reduced and is further diminished by increasingly frequent government intervention in employment problems. Nevertheless, the setting up of agreements binding a firm and its employees, from which disciplinary formalities emanate, should remain one of the chief concerns of higher management.

When discipline is violated, management must, for the well-being of the concern, apply certain sanctions capable of preventing or minimizing the recurrence of the incident. A manager's sense of proportion is well tested by the choice he makes of the sanction to be used and its degree, as he considers such alternatives as remonstrances, warnings, fines, suspension, transfer, demotion, and dismissal. The qualities of the individual involved and attendant circumstances must be taken into account. The employee should be given an opportunity to correct the mistake and offered help in doing so. Every step in the discipline process should be equitable, should reflect concern for the rights of the employee, and be free from any biases. All steps in the discipline process must be fully documented.

To sum up, discipline entails respect for agreements that are directed at achieving obedience, application, energy, and the outward marks of respect. Discipline should prevail just as much among managers at high levels as among the lowest-level employees, and the best means for establishing and maintaining it are as follows:

1) Having good superiors at all levels.
2) Making sure that the relevant agreements are as clear and fair as possible.
3) Behaving equitably and carefully documenting all steps of the discipline process.
4) Applying sanctions judiciously.

UNITY OF COMMAND

For any action whatsoever, an employee should receive orders from one superior only. Such is the rule of unity of command, which arises from general and ever-present necessity and wields a tremendous influence on the conduct of a business. Unity of command is threatened by technological change, which has brought about frequent separation between those who are knowledgeable about technical matters and those who are in a position in the hierarchy where they must make decisions concerning those matters. A subordinate could find himself receiving orders from a person with formal authority that contradict the "orders" from another individual who has superior knowledge about (or "functional" authority) over such matters. In such a case the person with formal authority is undermined, discipline may be put in jeopardy, order disturbed, and stability threatened. As soon as two superiors wield their authority over the same person or department—whether their authority arises from position, knowledge, or function—uneasiness is felt. Should the cause persist, the disorder increases, the department ails much in the manner of an animal organism troubled by a foreign body, and one of two consequences follows: either the dual command ends in disappearance or elimination of one of the superiors and organic well-being is restored, or, the organism continues to wither away. Cases of adaptation to dual command do occur, primarily in industries where the technology is extremely complex, where technology is rapidly changing, and where a sharp division can be drawn between functional supervision derived from knowledge and formal supervision derived from a place in the hierarchy. However, at best, the adaptation of the social organism is difficult and imperfect; management, therefore, must be continuously alert for ways of mitigating the discomforts that arise from the situation.

Dual command is extremely common in organizations for which it is not appropriate and wreaks havoc in such concerns. It worms its way into the social organism on the most plausible pretexts. For instance:

1) In the hope of being better understood, gaining time, or rapidly putting a stop to an undesirable practice, a superior $S2$ may give orders directly to an employee E without going through the superior $S1$. If this mistake is repeated, the result is dual command with all its consequences: hesitation on the part of the subordinate, irritation and dissatisfaction on the part of the superior who was set aside, and disorder in the work. It will be seen later, however, that it is sometimes possible to bypass the scalar chain while avoiding the drawbacks of dual command.

2) A desire to avoid the immediate necessity of dividing up authority, which is especially common when close colleagues, friends, or family members start up an enterprise, can result in dual command reigning at the top of a concern right from the outset. Exercising the same powers and having the same authority over the same people, the two managers end up inevitably with dual command and its consequences. Despite harsh lessons, instances of this sort are still numerous. New colleagues count on their mutual regard, common interest, and good sense to save them from conflict and serious disagreement; but, save for rare exceptions, this illusion is short-lived. First, awkwardness is felt, then a certain irritation, and, in time, if dual command continues, even hatred. The danger can be reduced, but not entirely banished, for between two superiors on the same footing, some question will always be ill-defined. It is riding for a fall to allow a business organization to operate with two superiors on equal footing whose duties and authority overlap.

3) Imperfect demarcation of departments also leads to dual command. When two superiors issue orders in a sphere which each thinks his own, this constitutes dual command.

4) There is an ever present danger of dual command when different departments are constantly linked up, when there is a natural intermeshing of functions, or when duties are poorly defined. In such a situation, if a knowledgeable superior does not put things in order, footholds are established that later upset and compromise the way the organization conducts its affairs.

In all human associations—in industry, commerce, government agencies, the army, the home—dual command can be a perpetual source of conflicts. The problem, therefore, has a special claim on the attention of superiors of all ranks.

UNITY OF DIRECTION

This principle is expressed as "one head and one plan for a group of activities having the same objective." It is the condition essential to unity of action, coordination of strength, and focusing of effort. A body with two heads is in the social as in the animal sphere a monster, and has difficulty surviving. Unity of direction (one head, one plan) must not be confused with unity of command (one employee to have orders from one superior only). Unity of direction is provided for by sound organization of the body corporate, whereas unity of command relates to how personnel function within the established organization. Unity of command cannot exist without unity of direction, but does not flow from it.

SUBORDINATION OF INDIVIDUAL INTEREST TO GENERAL INTEREST

In a business, the interests of one employee or group of employees should not prevail over those of the concern, just as the interests of the home should come before those of its members, and the interests of the state should prevail over those of one citizen or group of citizens.

It seems that such an admonition should not need calling to mind. But ignorance, ambition, selfishness, laziness, weakness, and all human passions tend to cause the general interests to be lost sight of in favor of individual interests, and a perpetual struggle has to be waged against this trend. Although individual and general interests are of different orders of concern, magnitude, and impact, nevertheless they confront each other and demand equal attention; means must be found to reconcile them. This represents one of the great difficulties of management. Means of effecting it are as follows:

1) Firmness and good example on the part of superiors.
2) Agreements that are as fair as possible.
3) Excellent supervision.
4) Instilling in each employee a strong sense of the operating philosophy and goals of the firm, the goals of his department, the goals of his group, and the goals of his job.
5) Equity in meeting the needs of individual members of the body corporate and their families, both on and off the job.

REMUNERATION OF PERSONNEL

Remuneration of personnel is the price of services rendered. It should be fair and, so far as possible, afford satisfaction to both employer and employee. In part, the rate of remuneration depends on circumstances largely beyond the employer's control and unrelated to the employee's worth, such as the cost of living, abundance or shortage of personnel, general business conditions, and the economic position of the business. Nevertheless, management has some leeway in determining the method of payment adopted. This choice, because it can exercise considerable influence on the progress of the business, is not only an extremely important decision, it is also a thorny problem. In practice, the decision has been made in various companies by officers in a wide variety of functions and at different levels of the hierarchy, choosing among hundreds of different pay plans; so far no pay plan has shown itself to be completely free of serious problems. What is generally looked for in the method of payment is that it:

1) assures fair remuneration—equitable for employees and the firm;
2) encourages productivity by rewarding well-directed effort;
3) is not subject to abuse;
4) is comprehensible and uniformly applicable to those affected.

Let us examine briefly the modes of payment in use for compensating employees at various levels within the body corporate.

Time, Job, and Piece Rates

The basic modes of payment in use for workers are time rates, job rates, and piece rates. These three modes may be combined and important variations may be introduced through the provision of bonuses, profit-sharing schemes, fringe benefits, and nonfinancial incentives.

Time Rates: Under this system the workman sells the employer, in return for a predetermined sum, a specific period of work under defined conditions. The time can be a day, a week, a month, a year, or more. Casual or temporary employees will expect to have their services engaged by the day, those in the plant by the week, office workers by the month, and professional or business specialists, on salary by the year. This system is universal in offices and is the only workable method of payment where the work done is not susceptible to measurement.

Job Rates: Here the payment made depends on the execution of a definite job set in advance and may be independent of the length of the job. When payment is due only on the condition that the job is completed during the normal work period, this method merges into the time-rate method. When payment is made by daily job, supervision does not have to be as close as with payment by the day, but this has the drawback of leveling the output of good workers down to that of mediocre ones—they will complete the job and no more. The good ones are underutilized because they really could accomplish more; the mediocre ones usually complain that the task set is too heavy.

Piece Rates: Here, payment is related to work done and there is usually no limit. This system is often used in workshops where a large number of similar articles has to be made. It is found where individual productivity can be measured by number, weight, length, or other concrete attribute, and is used in a very wide variety of industries. The piece-rate method is often criticized on the grounds that it emphasizes quantity at the expense of quality and provokes disagreements when rates have to be revised in the light of manufacturing improvements. Piecework becomes contract work when applied to a specific quantity of units destined for a particular job or "contract." When the pieces are complex, or the rate per piece cannot be predetermined accurately, or the reject rate is likely to be high, the contractor accepting the job must still assure some payment to the workers and some funds for continued operation of the business. In such a case, to reduce the contractor's risk, there would be added to the contract piece price a payment for each day's work done.

Generally, piece rates give rise to increased earnings for the employee who can work quickly and efficiently and meet the quality standards. The method penalizes the employee who is slower or has a high reject rate. Because it ties payments so directly to output, those employees who cannot meet standards or earn a respectable wage should immediately be retrained. If this does not rectify the situation and changes in the methodology are not feasible, such employees should be reassigned to other work more suitable to their abilities.

The above three modes of payment are found in all large concerns; sometimes time rates prevail, sometimes one of the other two. In a workshop one workman may sometimes work on piece rates, sometimes on time rates. Each of these methods has its advantages and drawbacks, and its effectiveness will depend on circumstances and the abilities of superiors. No method of payment absolves management from possessing competence and the oft-mentioned sense of proportion; these are qualities upon which the productivity of workers and the peaceful atmosphere of the workshop will largely depend.

Bonuses

To arouse the worker's interest in the smooth running of the business, sometimes an increment in the form of a bonus is added to the time, job, or piece rate. In the shop, a bonus may be earned for high quality, hard work, freedom from machine breakdown, output, cleanliness, and so forth. Elsewhere, bonuses may be added to monthly or yearly salaries for meritorious performance on a particularly important assignment, for performance at a very high level on the general run of assignments, or for performance that exhibited unusual character attributes. Other systems establish a certain fixed relationship between the prosperity of the firm and the workers' wages or salaries. For example, some stock trading firms that are doing well have given bonuses equal to several months' salary for their workers. Bonuses may vary greatly in their nature, size, and qualifying conditions. In developing a bonus system, there are few limitations beyond those of human ingenuity and the discretion of management vis-à-vis the investors.

Bonuses may also be used in place of salary merit increases. A major problem in rewarding a worker's outstanding success over the past year with a sharp increase in salary for the years following is that his performance may not be sustained. Whether this drop in performance is a regression to the average output that is normally feasible, or it represents a slackening of the worker's efforts, or results from circumstances beyond his control, the firm that has granted a salary increase cannot reasonably "take it away" at the next downturn. Workers expect continuous growth in salary; this year's merit increase is the base from which next year's salary increase is to be considered, and decreases are often resisted even when the firm's fortunes take an unexpected downturn. A bonus, in contrast, can be given as a separate payment, labeled very carefully as the recognition for a specific performance, and identified as not a part of the salary or any forthcoming increases in that base. If the employee does not regard the bonus as a fixed increment to his income, he will be less likely to inflate his expenditures, and in years when no bonus is given he will be disappointed, but theoretically will not have fallen into financial difficulty.

Profit Sharing

For Workers: The idea of providing workers with a share of a firm's profits is a very attractive one, and it would seem that it is from such a system that harmony between capital and labor should come. But a good practical formula for such sharing has not yet been found. In large concerns, efforts to provide workers with profit sharing have often come up against insurmountable difficulties. First, profit sharing cannot exist in enterprises having no monetary objective (e.g., state services, religious or philanthropic organizations, scientific societies) and it is not possible in businesses that are running at a loss. Thus, profit sharing is excluded from a great number of concerns. There remain the prosperous business concerns, and in these organizations the desire to reconcile workers' and employers' interests is severely tested in the face of competition from low-cost imports, the high costs of capital, the need to meet technological change with expensive research, the need to keep the firm's productive assets at the cutting edge of technology, and the need to declare a reasonable dividend to the investors.

Whether a business is making a profit or not, the worker must have an immediate wage assured to him; a system that would make workers' payments depend entirely on eventual future profit is unworkable. In addition, an individual worker's greater or lesser contribution to the final outcome of a large concern is extremely difficult to assess, unless the firm has established comprehensive systems for tracking that contribution. A firm that does the latter must devote substantial resources to the process of determining what each worker has done and how his accomplishments have contributed to the overall good of the firm. Alternatively, the firm may track the contributions made by groups, departments, or whole divisions and entirely bypass the question of what each individual has done. This, however, is equivalent to treating each employee's contribution within that unit as equal to that of any other employee and may lead outstanding employees to lessen their efforts, lead mediocre employees to coast on the work of others, and cause performance to settle down to a minimally satisfactory level.

Some firms sidestep this problem by tying profit sharing to cost savings which can be attributed to the activities of a sufficiently small subgroup so that performance leveling is not likely to occur. Still other firms tie profit sharing to the overall amount of dollar savings, increases in productivity, increases in profits, or reductions in resources used; the savings are split between the firm and the workers, with the latter receiving their share in the form of a percentage added to base pay. Unfortunately, such plans usually do not work beyond a few years. Savings can be achieved in any organization or activity by cutting "fat," eliminating redundant efforts, and so on, but for how long is it possible to keep finding places to improve? In the first few years, the shares of profits are satisfying and greeted with joy, but almost by definition, a successful cost-savings program puts itself out of business after a while—most of the feasible ideas have been exhausted. Then the amounts available for profit sharing shrink and disappear. Significantly, few large concerns have real profit-sharing programs operating, and many installed them when the firm got into serious financial difficulties and the profit-sharing system was a way of deferring wage increases. In many situations, the profit-sharing payments amount to bonuses in disguise; management unexpectedly finds that profits are exceptionally large and shares with employees in order to demonstrate management's continued attention to performance and its tie to the equity of their remuneration. Under such a payment plan, any other conditions, such as a period of moderate profitability, generally yield no distribution of profits to workers.

For Junior Managers: Profit sharing for foremen, superintendents, professionals, and the managers of the various overhead functions is scarcely more advanced than for workers. Nevertheless, the influence of these employees on the results of a business can be considerable, and if they seem uninterested in profit sharing, the only reason is that the basis for their participation in any plan is very difficult to establish. Such "lack of interest" is easy to counter: they are not indifferent to extra income and an equitable profit-sharing plan can arouse their enthusiasm and induce a strong interest in the company's performance. This is relatively easy in businesses that are just starting out, in which exceptional effort can yield outstanding results. In such cases, junior managers may share in overall business profits or may be rewarded for the successful running of a particular department. As the business matures, however, and maintains itself as a well-run organization, the zeal of an individual junior manager, unless he is in a truly strategic position, is scarcely apparent in the general outcome. It is very hard to establish a useful basis on which he may participate individually in direct proportion to his contribution. Therefore, in large concerns, profit sharing for middle-level managers is relatively rare. Production or performance bonuses—not to be confused with profit sharing—are much more common.

For Higher Level Managers: It is necessary to go right up to top management to find a class of employee with constant interest in the profits of the large-scale concern. The head of the business, through his knowledge, ideas, and actions, exerts considerable influence on general results, so it is quite natural to try to provide him with a monetary interest in them. Sometimes it is possible to establish a close connection between his personal activity and its effects. Nevertheless, generally speaking, other influences quite independent of the personal capability of the manager can influence results to a greater extent than can his personal activity. If the manager's salary were exclusively dependent upon profits, it might at times be reduced to nothing. Besides, in businesses that are being built up, being phased out, or merely passing through a temporary crisis, management talent is needed just as much as in prosperous concerns, yet profit sharing is not a reasonable basis for remuneration for the top manager. And profit sharing is obviously impossible for senior civil servants or others who work in nonprofit organizations.

Profit sharing then, for either higher managers or workers, is not the general mode of remuneration. Rather, the board of directors will award higher level managers with bonuses which, while keyed to the level of profits, do not actually constitute profit sharing. To sum up, profit sharing is a mode of payment capable of giving excellent results in certain cases, but is not the general rule for remuneration.

Perquisites, Provision for Employee Welfare, Nonfinancial Incentives

Whether an employee's earnings consist solely of money, or whether they include various perquisites or extras such as housing and automobiles, is of little consequence provided that the employee is satisfied.

Clearly, a business is best served when its employees are energetic, well educated, conscientious, and permanent. Accordingly, the employer should be concerned, if merely in the interests of the business, with the health, education, morale, and stability of his personnel. These elements, which all contribute to the smooth running of the concern, are not acquired in the plant or workshop alone. They are formed and developed, as well, outside of the company—in the home and school, in community and religious life. Therefore, the employer comes to be concerned with the personal lives of his employees. Here the question of proportion comes up again: opinion is greatly divided on the degree of involvement that an employer should have in such matters. Some employers stop short their interest at the works gate; their duty to the employee is deemed ended with the payment of wages for the work done and the provision of a minimal level of fringe benefits. The majority believe that the employer's interests in the employees should extend to good purpose outside the factory confines provided that discretion and prudence are exercised, that the employer's involvement is sought after rather than imposed, that it is exercised in a manner which respects the intelligence and capabilities of those concerned, and that the employer has absolute respect for the employees' liberty. There must be benevolent collaboration, not tyrannical stewardship, and management must retain flexibility in attempting to advance the welfare of employees.

Activities designed to promote the employee's welfare may be of various kinds. In the plant or workshop, they bear on matters of hygiene, comfort, ventilation, lighting, safety, canteen facilities, and general working conditions. Outside the workplace, they bear on medical protection for the employee and family, life insurance, education, special training, and even aid with housing and transportation. In a more general sense, the firm promotes the welfare of employees by serving the community as a good corporate citizen, generously seeking to make the community a better place in which to live.

Nonfinancial incentives are also key elements in attracting and retaining the best and the brightest employees. Such incentives help allay employee fears of calamity, make it easier for the employees to concentrate on the work because basic family needs are being met, and make the employees' lives outside the workplace richer. At the very least, nonfinancial incentives improve morale and productivity of employees at all levels. Such incentives, without doubt, have been found to provide immense benefits for the employer, and therefore should be a matter for managers' constant review.

CENTRALIZATION

Like division of work, centralization belongs to the natural order: in every organism, animal or social, sensations converge toward the brain or directive part, and from the brain or directive part, orders are sent out that set all parts of the organism in movement. Centralization is not a system of management that can be completely adopted or completely discarded, depending on the whims of managers or on circumstances; rather, in any organization, it is always present to a greater or lesser extent. The issue of centralization versus decentralization is simply one of proportion; it is a matter of finding the optimum degree of centralization for the particular concern. In small firms, where the manager's orders go directly to subordinates, there is absolute centralization; in large concerns, where a long scalar chain is interposed between top managers and the lower grades, orders and information have to go through a series of intermediaries. Each employee, intentionally or unintentionally, puts something of himself into the transmission of information and the execution of orders. He does not operate merely as a cog in a machine. Everything which goes to increase the importance of the subordinate's role is decentralization; everything that serves to reduce it is centralization. The degree of initiative that an intermediary may exercise depends on his personal character and moral worth, and on the reliability of his own subordinates, the character of his own superior, and the condition of the business. The degree of centralization that is appropriate varies with the firm. The objectives to pursue are the optimum utilization of all qualities of the personnel and the best overall yield for the concern.

If the top manager's moral worth, intelligence, experience, and swiftness of thought allow him to be proficient at leading a wide span of activities, he will be able to carry centralization quite far and reduce his seconds in command to mere executive agents. If, conversely, he prefers to have greater recourse to the experience, opinions, and counsel of his colleagues while reserving to himself the privilege of giving general directives, he can effect considerable decentralization.

Since the roles and contributions of top managers and lower level employees are constantly changing, it is understandable that the degree of centralization or decentralization may also vary constantly. The problem of how much to centralize activities is best solved according to circumstances: management should seek a scheme that will best satisfy the interests of all involved. The issue of centralization versus decentralization arises not only in the case of top management, but for superiors at all levels and has major ramifications for determining the extent of a subordinate's initiative and commitment to the decisions made.

SCALAR CHAIN

The scalar chain is the chain of superiors in a firm ranging from the ultimate authority to the lowest ranks. The line of authority is the route followed—via every link in the chain—by all communications that occur, whether they start from or go up to the top authority. This path is dictated both by the need to transmit information and by the principle of unity of command, but it is not always the swiftest. It is even at times disastrously lengthy in large concerns, notably in governmental ones. Since the success of many activities depends on speedy implementation of plans or speedy response to a situation, respect for the line of authority must be reconciled with the need for swift action.

Let us imagine that section F has to be put into contact with section P in a business whose scalar chain is represented by the following double ladder:

```
              A
           B     L
           C     M
           D     N
           E        O
           F－－－－－P
        G              Q
```

If the line of authority is followed, the ladder must be climbed from F to A and then descended from A to P, with a stop at each rung, then ascended again from P to A, and descended once more from A to F, in order to get back to the starting point. It is much simpler and quicker to go directly from F to P by making use of a direct interaction FP as a "gangplank," and that is what is most often done. The scalar principle will be safeguarded if managers E and O have authorized their respective subordinates F and P to deal with each other directly, and if F and P inform their respective superiors forthwith of what they have agreed upon. As long as F and P keep their superiors informed, and as long as the superiors continue to approve their actions, direct contact may be maintained. But from the instant there is no approval from the superiors, direct contact comes to an end, and the scalar chain is immediately resumed.

Such is the procedure followed in the great majority of businesses. It provides for the usual exercise of some measure of initiative at all levels of authority. The system works well only if employees are informed about the firm's objectives and keep them in mind. Breaking the scalar chain with cross interactions can result in too many people on the top rungs being uninformed about important matters. But, it furthers the interests of the firm for employees to be allowed to interact as opposed to being required to go through the chain as long as they keep the top informed. It takes knowledgeable employees to decide when to break the chain, when to inform management, and how to assure that top levels are not left out of the information flow. In the small concern, the general interest—that is, the interest of the concern proper—is easy to grasp, and the employer is present to recall this interest to those tempted to lose sight of it. In governments, very large organizations, or nonprofit service-oriented organizations, the general interest is such a complex, vast, remote element that it is not easy to get a clear idea of what it is. The firm's objectives become blurred and weakened unless they are constantly revived by top management through careful indoctrination, communication, and example. Where this is not done, each section comes to regard itself as its own aim and end; it forgets that it is only a cog in a big machine, all of whose parts must work in concert. Section personnel go about their business in an isolated manner, contact whomever they please, whenever they please, and overlook the necessity to keep the people in the line of authority and responsibility—the scalar chain—informed. The example provided by one department will soon be emulated by others, each of which winds up taking its own very narrow, constricted approach to accomplishing the business of the firm.

The use of the "gangplank" is simple, swift, and sure. It allows the two employees F and P to deal at one sitting, in a few hours, with some question which via the scalar chain would consume a vast amount of time and other resources. An issue traveling the chain would pass through 20 transmissions, inconvenience many people, involve masses of paper, lose weeks or months, and get to a conclusion less satisfactory than the one which could have been obtained via direct contact between F and P.

Is it possible that there are organizations which not only encourage the lengthy route, but forbid a contact between F and P? Unfortunately, there is little doubt that this is the case in some governmental agencies, some of the larger corporations that stress "correct" procedures, and some nonprofit agencies that make following protocol an elaborate part of their existence. This is a common phenomenon in an organization permeated by fear of responsibility—a fear which is quite frequently rooted in inadequate leadership capacity on the part of those in charge. If, however, supreme authority A insisted that his assistants B and L made use of the "gangplank" themselves, and likewise made its use incumbent upon their subordinates C and M, this would establish both the habit of taking responsibility and the custom of using the shortest path to get the job done.

It is an error to depart needlessly from the line of authority, but it is an even greater one to keep to it when detriment to the business ensues. The latter may sometimes attain extreme gravity. When an employee is obliged to choose between the two practices, and advice from his superior is not forthcoming, he should be courageous enough and feel free enough to adopt whichever practice seems dictated by the objectives of the firm. But for him to be in this frame of mind, there must have been previous precedent, and his superiors must have set the example, for example must always come from above.

ORDER

The formula for order in the case of material things is "a place for everything and everything in its place." The formula in the human order is "a place for everyone and everyone in his place."

Material Order

As indicated above, if material order is to prevail, there must be a place appointed for each thing and each thing must be in its appointed place. Is that enough? Is it not also necessary that the place should have been well chosen? The objective of order is to avoid losses of material and time, and for these objectives to be completely realized, not only must things be in their places suitably arranged, but the places must have been chosen so as to facilitate all activities as much as possible. If this last condition is unfulfilled, there is merely the appearance of order—an appearance that may cover over true disorder. For example, a works yard used as a storage place for steel ingots gave a pleasing impression of orderliness: the material was well stacked, evenly arranged, and clean. On closer inspection, however, it was noted that the same heap included five or six types of steel, intended for different manufacturing operations, all mixed together. The result: useless handling, lost time, and risk of mistakes because each thing was not in its place.

The opposite situation may also occur, in that the appearance of disorder may actually reflect true order. Such is the case with papers, tools, or parts scattered about on a technician's workbench which a well-meaning supervisor orders rearranged and stacked in neat piles. The technician may then no longer know where everything is. Perfect order presupposes a judiciously chosen place and the appearance of order is merely a false or imperfect image of real order.

Social Order

For social order to prevail in a concern, there must be an appointed place for every employee, and every employee must be in his appointed place. Perfect order requires, furthermore, that the place be suitable for the employee and the employee for the place: "the right man in the right place."

Social order presupposes the successful execution of the two most difficult managerial activities: good organization and good selection of personnel. It might at first glance appear that once the posts essential to the smooth running of the business have been decided upon, and those who will fill such posts have been selected, each employee now occupies that post wherein he can render most service. Perfect social order would be deemed to be in operation—"a place for each one and each one in his place"—and we might conjure up immediately a concept of perfect administration. This is a mirage, however.

Social order demands precise knowledge of the human requirements and resources of the concern and a constant balance between these requirements and resources. This balance is very difficult to establish and maintain, and becomes even more difficult the bigger the business. When the balance has been upset and the pursuit of individual interests has resulted in neglect or sacrifice of the general interest—when management, acting out of ambition, nepotism, favoritism, or merely ignorance has multiplied positions without good reason or filled them with incompetent employees—then drastic action is called for. Management will need to draw on its special reservoirs of talent, strength of will, and persistence in order to sweep away abuses and restore order.

The principle of "a place for each one and each one in his place" has great breadth. It means that the organization must carefully map out the needs it will have for each type of position while, at the same time, it supports career planning for the employees who will be needed to fill those positions. The process of defining new positions, monitoring how changes in technology will affect the performance of different jobs, assessing the need for special training of managers, developing the skills of employees, preventing obsolescence of skills, and determining the line of succession is called organization development. The aim of this process is to ensure that each employee finds a position in the firm that benefits it to the maximum extent while meeting the employee's need for career development. As in the case of orderly material arrangement, charts or plans facilitate the establishment and control of human arrangements. Such charts show the firm's personnel in their entirety, indicating which positions are promotional steps to other positions, which positions are good training for higher management, and which positions call for special talents that must be supplied as the firm grows. Such charts should also show the individuals who are currently in the positions, their present duties, and the potential of each person for a broadening of responsibilities, advancement, or even separation from the firm when the current workload is completed.

EQUITY

Why the term "equity" rather than "justice"? Justice means putting into execution established conventions, but conventions cannot foresee everything; they need to be interpreted and at times supplemented by actions that recognize the dignity and worth of the employees. For personnel to be encouraged to carry out their duties with all the devotion and loyalty of which they are capable, they must be treated with respect for their own sense of integrity, and equity results from the combination of respect and justice. Equity excludes neither forcefulness nor sternness, but rather involves the application of these qualities in proportion, with good sense and good nature.

The desire for equity and equality of treatment must always be taken into account in management's dealings with employees. In order to achieve equity as much as possible without neglecting any principle of management or losing sight of the general interest, the head of the business must frequently summon up his highest faculties. He should strive to instill a sense of equity throughout all levels of the scalar chain.

STABILITY OF TENURE OF PERSONNEL

Time is required for an employee to get used to new work and succeed in doing it well, assuming that he possesses the requisite abilities. If he is terminated before he has gotten used to the work, he will not have had time to render worthwhile service. Such insecurity of tenure has especially undesirable consequences in large concerns, where it generally takes considerable time for managers to settle into their work. Indeed, much time is needed if a new manager is to get to know the people and material resources of a department to the point where he will be able to decide on a plan of action, gain confidence in himself, and inspire confidence in others. Hence, there are many instances in which a mediocre manager who stays is preferable to outstanding managers who merely come and go.

Generally, the managerial personnel of prosperous concerns are stable, and those of unsuccessful ones are unstable. Instability of tenure is simultaneously the cause and the effect of mediocrity in operations and should, therefore, be minimized. However, it must be kept in mind that like all the other principles of management, stability of tenure of personnel is also a matter of proportion. While instability of tenure is generally undesirable, it can be costly to retain employees who continue in positions without pulling their full weight for the business, and for a higher manager the cost is generally even greater. Mindless emphasis on the elimination of all turnover could multiply these costs and result in stagnation for the firm. Some changes of personnel are inevitable: age, illness, retirement, and death will periodically disturb the human makeup of the firm. Other employees may become incapable of carrying out their duties: perhaps their jobs have changed and they have not adapted, or they themselves have changed and can no longer perform as in the past—so reassignment or separation may be necessary. Still other employees may have become fit to assume greater responsibilities. Between too little turnover (too great a stability of personnel) and too much turnover (too little stability of personnel), each firm must decide for itself the appropriate proportions. This decision should be made on the basis of careful management consideration, not by default—acceptance of what happens by chance.

INITIATIVE

Thinking out a plan and ensuring its success are two of the keenest satisfactions that an intelligent person can experience. The opportunity to plan and implement is also one of the most powerful stimulants of human endeavor. Thus, the manager who allows and encourages employees to exercise initiative—that is, propose plans and take an active role in their implementation—is tapping a substantial reservoir of human potential. At all levels of the organizational ladder, zeal and energy on the part of employees are augmented by initiative. The initiative of all employees, added to that of the manager, represents a great source of strength for a business. This is particularly apparent in difficult times; hence, it is essential to encourage and develop this capacity to the fullest.

Much tact and some integrity are required to inspire and maintain everyone's initiative within the limits imposed by the need for respect and discipline. The manager must be able to sacrifice some personal vanity in order to grant this sort of satisfaction to subordinates. Other things being equal, a manager who permits the exercise of initiative on the part of subordinates is infinitely superior to one who does not do so.

ESPRIT DE CORPS

"Union is strength." Heads of business would do well to ponder this proverb. Union among the personnel of a concern, exemplified by harmonious working relationships and a commitment to common goals, is a great strength of that concern. Considerable effort, then, should be made to establish it. Among the countless methods in use, we will single out one principle that especially needs to be observed and two pitfalls to be avoided. The principle to be observed is unity of command, which was previously covered in detail. The dangers to be avoided—the splitting up of personnel and the abuse of written communications—are explained as follows.

1) Personnel should not be split up. Some managers are led astray by a misguided interpretation of the motto "divide and rule." Dividing enemy forces to weaken them is clever, but dividing one's own team is a grave sin against the business. Whether this error results from inadequate managerial capacity, from an imperfect grasp of present conditions, or from egotism that sacrifices general interest to personal interest, it is always reprehensible because it is harmful to the business. There is no special knack needed to sow dissension among subordinates; any beginner can do it. Where real talent comes into play is in coordinating individual efforts, encouraging employees to do good work, making the best use of each person's abilities, and rewarding each person's merit without arousing possible jealousies and disturbing harmonious relations.

2) Abuse of written communications. In dealing with a business problem or giving an order that involves some explanation, it is usually simpler and quicker to do so orally than in writing. Additionally, differences and misunderstandings that a conversation could clear up grow more protracted and even bitter in writing. Therefore, wherever possible, communications should be oral; there is a gain in speed, clarity, instant response, and harmony.

In some firms, employees of neighboring departments who come in contact with one another frequently, or even employees within the same department who could quite easily get together, communicate with each other only in writing. Too many of these communications are grounded in fear—the writer believes that the memo will cover his actions should anything go wrong. Consequently, the contents, phrasing, and timing of the notes are all designed not to get the business of the firm done, but rather to protect the writer. The result may be an increase in unnecessary work, complications, and delays that are harmful to the business, or the prevalence of a certain animosity between different departments or between different employees within a department. A system where most communications are written, stemming as it often does from individual insecurities, usually brings many negative consequences. To put an end to such a system, management should set a strong example of discouraging any communications in writing that could easily and advantageously be replaced by oral ones. Here again, though, the question of proportion arises. Management will not want to eliminate all written communications, but only those that seem counterproductive.

It is not merely by satisfactory results that the power of unity is demonstrated. In a firm where unity and an esprit de corps prevail, each employee knows what his job is, knows what outcome of that job will best benefit the business, and knows how to mesh his efforts with those around him to achieve the firm's aims. Superiors allow their subordinates to have the degree of authority necessary to get things done, charge the subordinates with the responsibility for accomplishing those things, and properly reward (or punish) them for the results achieved. When an employee finds that he has real input into management decision making, that his efforts are properly directed, and that his output is highly valued, he becomes committed to the firm and its work. He develops a loyalty to management and a commitment to achieving its aims. Such unity will spread to the agreements between employer and employee, between employer and unions, between owners and executives, and, finally, between employer and associations of every kind that affect the affairs of the business.

SUMMARY

This brings us to the end of the review of the principles of management, not because the list is exhausted—it really has no precise limits—but because the principles outlined seem to be the ones that are basic to nearly all others. These principles, which inject a sense of direction into the management process, form almost a code by which the managers can make best use of the body corporate. This code is indispensable. In every concern—be it commercial, industrial, political, religious, military, or philanthropic—there is a management function to be performed, and for proper performance, there must be principles: acknowledged truths upon which to rely. The managerial code, made up of the principles of management, represents the sum total of these truths at any given moment.

It might at first seem surprising that the eternal moral principles, the commandments of the Bible, are not a sufficient guide for the manager and that a special code is needed. The explanation is this: the higher laws of religion or moral order encompass the individual's place in society as a whole and form broad boundaries within which all human endeavor takes place. Management principles operate on a narrow scope within these boundaries—they aim at the success of organizations of individuals and at the satisfaction of economic interests. Given that the scopes are different, it is not surprising that the principles are set down so specifically in the case of the economic organization. There is no contradiction between the codes of religion and the codes of business, as the latter lie within the bounds of the former—it is a question, again, of proportion. Without the larger principles one is in darkness and chaos; without the more specific principles one is handicapped in the performance of the management process. The principles, in both cases, are the lighthouses giving the bearings, but they can only serve those who are willing to be guided by them into port.

9 The Various Abilities Needed by a Firm's Personnel

For every group of activities or essential functions, there exists a corresponding special ability. These abilities may be technical, commercial, financial, managerial, and so forth. Each ability is based on a combination of qualities and of knowledge, which may be summarized as follows:

1) Physical qualities: health, vigor, bearing.

2) Mental qualities: ability to understand and learn, ability to integrate experiences into a coherent body of knowledge, judgment, mental agility, and adaptability.

3) Moral qualities: energy, firmness, willingness to accept responsibility, initiative, loyalty, tact, dignity, ethics.

4) General education: general acquaintance with matters not related exclusively to the function performed, a broad background that enables one to adapt to changes in society and to comprehend a wide variety of business matters.

5) Special knowledge: that peculiar to the function, be it technical, commercial, financial, managerial, or other.

6) Experience: knowledge arising from the work proper that is of increasing breadth, depth, and amount as the challenge of the work increases. Experience is the recollection of lessons that one has derived from business events.

7) The greatest possible competence in the specialized activities that represent the raison d'être of the concern.

Interestingly, the first six of these qualities apply regardless of the nature of the enterprise; only one, the seventh, will involve special features that vary with the type of concern. Leaders of comparable rank in industry, commerce, politics, the military, and religion are alike insofar as the first six categories go, and differ only in the terms of the specialized area of competence they bring to the enterprise. Most men who have become leaders of enterprises first attracted attention by their specialized ability: their impressive mastery of their function first distinguished them from their peers, and then, later, their general abilities carried them to the forefront. Many observers may see in the outstanding industrialist merely the eminent technical man, or in the head of a government merely the successful general or eloquent parliamentarian. However, this view is shortsighted; the most brilliant specialized ability is not enough to make someone a top-notch manager of a large concern. In a "perfect leader," all the above mentioned qualities are present to a high degree.

People who come close to such perfection are hardly common. Weaknesses and shortcomings must be expected and allowed, but to what extent? Bad health or inadequate mental powers may nullify all the other qualities taken together. General managerial ability is a necessity: in special cases, detailed knowledge about a given function (even the one that constitutes the primary activity of the business) may be largely supplied via departmental heads and the staff, but nothing can make up for lack of managerial ability. Finally, a word should be included about the manager as a role model. Employees at all levels under a particular officer of the firm take their behavior and performance cues from him; the manager's behavior must meet the highest professional standards. This must be especially emphasized in the area of moral behavior. Moral flaws on the part of a higher level manager can lead to serious consequences, for a high position in the scalar chain is like the arm of a lever whose length increases its power considerably; good and bad qualities are a hundred times more important in a seven- or eight-striped leader than in a foreman.

EMPLOYEE CHARACTERISTICS

Managers

The qualities that the head of a business should possess will depend on the role to be played by that individual, on the firm's main activities, and on the type of supporting staff to be assembled. If the firm's major problems are perceived to be in dealing with government, the head of the business may be chosen from the legal ranks of the corporation. If the firm faces difficult decisions about the marketing of its products, the top manager might be imported, if necessary, from a successful marketing firm to work his "magic" on his new affiliation's products. Similar logic would apply if the main challenge is perceived to be in engineering or the financial area. The head of the business should seek a supporting staff that will support his strengths, make up for his weaknesses, and, at the same time, ensure that no area, internal or external, of importance to the firm is neglected.

The ideal manager would be one who, possessed of all requisite knowledge for settling managerial, technical, commercial, financial, and other questions that are brought to his attention, also enjoyed sufficient physical and mental vigor to be able to carry the entire weight of business contacts with the outside world as well as the internal functions incumbent upon management. Such people might be found once in a while in small concerns; they are not likely to be found in large businesses, and especially not in the very largest ones. There is no single person whose knowledge embraces every question that will arise in the running of a large concern, and certainly none who has enough energy and time to attend to every one of the manifold obligations of large-scale management. Hence the need to fall back on the staff, wherein lies a reserve of physical and mental energies, competence, and time contribution on which the manager can draw at will.

The person who builds a career with a firm, as it grows from small to medium to large, must be able to accept an increasing separation between himself and the technical details of the function in which he initially concentrated. At first, he may do the actual production or the performance of the service for which the firm earns its revenue. He may also do specialty functions such as accounting, selling, or handling the firm's flow of funds. As the work grows, and the staff that performs it does likewise, he will need to stop doing the actual detail work involved in the function and, instead, will manage the people doing the work. This shift requires a major change in the "mind set" of the individual concerned; all too often, the individual assumes the managerial duties but is unable to let go of the technical details. He fears instant obsolescence, loss of a tangible output by which he can be measured, and a variety of other "threats" to his career. It is a major duty of the firm to understand these threats, relieve them, and train the individual in how to properly assume the managerial duties.

As the firm grows further, the manager will find that the work which needs to be done is overwhelming the staff. Functional specialties now require subunits, which result in the interspersing of further levels of management between the rising manager and those who actually perform the work. At this point, the handling of the firm's affairs involves managing people who, in turn, manage others who, again in turn, manage those doing the work. The job becomes more managerial as it becomes more remote from the technical work. The technical function, which was predominant in the small firm, is downgraded in priority as the firm grows—the other specialties begin to absorb the chief's time and attention; layers of management start building to handle the volume of work and the increased scope of operations. The head of the firm can no longer have the luxury of dabbling in the technical details of the product or in the specialty that was his original point of entry into the business.

Between the qualities and knowledge essential on the part of the head of a large concern (even the head of a government) and those qualities and knowledge essential for an artisan who is the sole worker in his business or trade, there are merely differences of degree. The same elements are needed in the total make-up of each type of manager, but the elements are combined in different proportions. In the case of the manager of a large concern, general managerial capacity is most important; in fact, it outweighs in importance all the other abilities taken together. (Total lack of one of the secondary abilities can be a serious handicap to

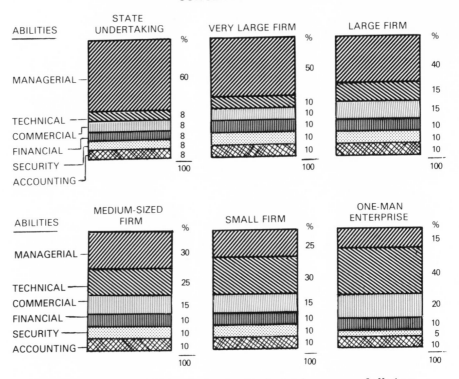

REQUISITE ABILITIES FOR HEADS OF INDUSTRIAL CONCERNS OF ALL SIZES

Fig. 4. Requisite abilities for heads of industrial concerns of all sizes.

such a manager, but he may be able to remedy the problem via his staff.) For the head of the one-man business, technical capacity in the specialized activity of the business is first in importance; the commercial and financial abilities are a strong second and third, respectively. Fig. 4 shows the gradual changes that occur in the relative importance of the various functional abilities as a business expands or contracts. Note that these proportions are only generalizations and that, in terms of specific skills exercised, there is scarcely anything in common between each ability in the case of the one-man head and the same ability in the case of the higher manager.

Departmental Heads

Under a series of superiors $S1, S2, S3, S4, \cdots, Sn$ would be found a series of departmental heads $SD1, SD2, SD3, \cdots, SDn$. The managers of the whole concern are responsible for that whole and must see that all functions are performed, whereas the responsibility of departmental managers extends only over a portion of the concern. As Fig. 5 shows, de-

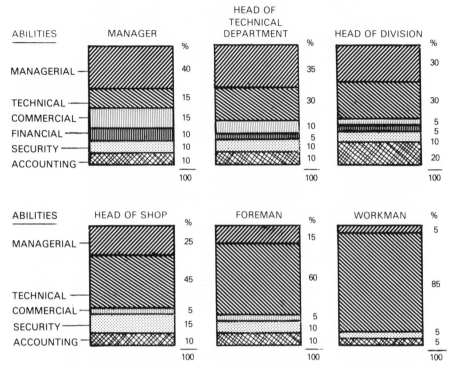

REQUISITE ABILITIES FOR PERSONNEL OF THE TECHNICAL FUNCTION OF A LARGE CONCERN

Fig. 5. Requisite abilities for personnel of the technical function of a large concern.

partmental managers need to have the same abilities as heads of businesses, only in different proportions.

Lower Grades—Operatives

The functional abilities needed at the lower grades of the business become heavily oriented toward the technical as shown in Fig. 5. At the lowest levels, accounting and financial abilities are not requisite. When operatives encounter these functions, it is through the use of carefully structured systems; performance is by rote only. The essential personal qualities and knowledge that were previously listed for higher level employees (health, intelligence, etc.) hold true for the operatives as well. But the degree of competence in each area and the depth of knowledge required are certainly not as great on the operative level.

To demonstrate this, let us take an expanded look at the essential personal qualities needed as one moves up the hierarchy from operative to higher manager. As noted earlier, the qualities include:

1) Health and Physical Fitness: These qualities are essential at all ranks within an enterprise, from operative to top manager. One might expect that the operatives who do physical work would develop stronger bodies and therefore be more physically fit, but it should also be remembered that the operative runs the greatest risk of developing a physical disability peculiar to his particular occupation. It is management's job to preserve the health and physical fitness of all workers, up and down the line, on and off the job. Management should provide health insurance, necessary training, proper working conditions, and encouragement for workers to take care of their health off the job as well.

2) Intelligence and Mental Vigor: Intelligence can be viewed as comprising judgement, memory, and ability to understand and assimilate information. Mental vigor makes it possible either to summon up all one's energies to solve an urgent problem, to deal simultaneously with a variety of subjects, or to simply follow complex procedures. Intelligence and mental vigor are increasingly necessary as the work embraces more numerous, widespread, and complex activities; the higher manager needs to have a substantial breadth of vision and great flexibility of mind. And, because of the increasing complexity of operating a business, in everything from human relations to the production processes themselves, it is equally important that workers at lower levels, even foremen, have a respectable breadth of vision and flexibility of mind. Such qualities are also increasingly needed in the work force since new technologies have made employees' work more demanding and complex.

3) Moral Qualities: The term "character" is frequently used to cover moral qualities such as drive, steadfastness, integrity, and initiative, in addition to the legal and ethical ramifications of the term. Discipline, integrity, and loyalty are expected of all industrial employees of whatever rank. Initiative is a precious gift in everyone, but more useful the higher the rank. As for steadfastness, sense of proportion, and acceptance of responsibility, the importance of these qualities increases with one's level in the organization; they may be set at the head of the list of attributes needed in higher level managers. Importantly, moral qualities also encompass a worker's sense of duty, obligation, or allegiance to the mores of his country, community, profession, and the firm for which he works. It is not only the goal toward which one works that counts: in a society that expects moral behavior, the way in which a goal is reached is just as important as what is accomplished once there—the end cannot be said to justify the means if those means violated a moral duty.

4) General Education: This refers to the acquisition of general ideas that are not particular only to the sphere of a work function performed (the latter having been imparted through training). General education is acquired partly at school, partly from everyday life, and partly from the exercise of a healthy curiosity. People can be found with relatively less education than the norm who nevertheless have risen to high industrial, commercial, political, or military rank and whose knowledge has always been equal to the occasion. Still, everyone who rises high in an organization needs to improve his general education by reading great books, attending college courses, or engaging in intellectual exercises.

5) Special Knowledge: This knowledge is that peculiar to the function with which the person is engaged. At the lower levels, the function will be in one of the technical specialties or one of the staff operations. As one moves higher up the ranks, to management, that specialty evolves into a concentration on the basic process of management: planning, organizing, coordinating, commanding, and controlling. For operatives, the managerial abilities needed are elementary: managerial requirements widen as employees move to higher ranks. While theories about the management process might be learned at a university, and its practice even simulated in game situations, the management process is one in which empiricism reigns supreme. Just as the operative sharpens his skills by the everyday performance of his duties, the manager must sharpen his skills by the everyday experience and involvement in the operations of his organization.

6) Experience: Moving upward from operative to foreman to superintendent, and from higher executives to the general manager position of an industrial concern, it is apparent that the scope of the duties with which one must cope widens. Usually the operative has only one type of job, the foreman's supervisory work spans four or five, the superintendent's eight or nine, the executive's more. As for the general manager, he must have some conception not merely of the specialized technical activities of the concern, but also of its sweeping commercial, financial, and other interests. Competence to deal with all of these can only come with maturity. Maturity can only come with experience. The experience is tied together, integrated, by theory, but without the direct exposure to the situations which arise in daily operations, accumulated over a respectable period of time, the individual who moves up the ranks will find himself overwhelmed by the increasing scope of the matters with which he must deal.

This experience teaches him which details to disregard, which to consider in a peripheral manner, and which are of extreme importance. The person moving up the ranks may become detached from the specialized work insofar as ability to do it, and even to directly supervise it. But he must never become remote enough from the work performed by the body corporate that he can no longer assure himself, by direct observation when necessary, that it is being done properly.

It follows, then, that the foreman is usually less competent than each one of his workers at their particular jobs, that the superintendent is less competent than the foreman in the specialized work of each group, and that the department head is less competent than the superintendent within the latter's own sphere. The general manager can lay no claim to being any better than each of his departmental heads in their respective spheres, but he should have broad ideas about all departments. The scope of knowledge needed increases with rank.

7) Competence in Activities of the Business: This capacity, comprising almost the whole of how an operative's performance is evaluated, refers to his ability to actually turn out the assigned parts of the product, or to develop, assemble, test, sell, or deliver it. The operative, whether an engineer in a laboratory or a worker on a lathe, is the one doing the job for which the firm is being paid—turning out the product or service from which revenue is generated. The term "competence" does not only refer to an operative's hand or other physical skills; competence may also encompass mental skills or the operative's ability to integrate his mental and physical skills with the "intelligence" of the machine.

Moving back up the line, it is obvious that while understanding the technology of the business is important at all levels, the ability to turn the wheels of the actual production machinery is not. As one moves higher in the hierarchy, an orientation toward physical action turns into a cognitive orientation. Sometimes, though, there is a need for higher management to attend more closely to physical and technological matters. In industries where technology changes very quickly, higher managers should receive frequent briefings so that in making decisions they will not be totally dependent on the advice of staff or departmental heads.

Thus, for various abilities that are desirable in a firm's personnel, the lower levels are stronger in some while the top levels are stronger in others. It is the responsibility of top management to assure that the mix of abilities is the correct one for the firm and that the distribution of abilities by level makes the firm as effective and efficient as possible.

In the one-man business, where all activities are carried out by the same person, general management and operational activities are merged. In a slightly larger concern, the top person retains sole responsibility for properly managing the firm, but is relieved from carrying out many activities. As the concern grows, the operative aspects of the manager's work continue to diminish, while his function of managing becomes increasingly important and difficult (and deals with increasingly abstract elements, such as "information").

What has happened, in effect, is that the single-dimensional thinker has grown into a multidimensional head of a large firm. Each decision must be evaluated not only in terms of its effect on a single function, but also in terms of how it will damage or benefit all the other functions. In terms of our schools of thought, each decision must be evaluated not only in terms of the single school in which it is being made, but in terms of its impact on all the others as well. How does a person develop into a multidimensional thinker? This transition does not spring full blown from the mind of an individual at a set age, but rather is the product both of his development, in terms of the patterns of mental growth, and of the specialized teaching of management in the schools.

In the following material we will discuss how that development takes place—namely in the home, through the state, through general education, and through the efforts of the employer (who builds, in effect, on the contributions made by all the other sources). We will then focus more closely on the need for management teaching and will close with advice to university graduates looking forward to management careers.

EMPLOYEE DEVELOPMENT

The Place of the Home

The efficient employee has developed the proper habits, attentiveness, and willingness to work ever since birth. A home that is well managed, and places value on foresight, good organization, and efficient methods lays the foundation in its children for the entire process of management. In a natural manner, such a home instills principles into children's minds that will be further developed later on. The home may afford the most varied examples of how managerial principles are applied or fail to be applied; it may range from the best to the worst of operating organizations. Most importantly, however, the home fosters experimentation on the part of young people. They can try out different actions, reactions, and modes of "management" on different people with whom they come in contact, at different ages and under varying social circumstances. They learn by experience. Thus, it can be seen that in the well-managed home, development of appropriate and wide-ranging skills begins, indeed, from earliest consciousness.

The Place of the State

The state contributes to the managerial training of its citizens through its schools and by its own example. In the most important government agencies, the management process must be well performed if the citizens are to receive the maximum benefit from the agency programs. Whereas in the past, government service was for an elite few, present-day practices have opened up everything from operative to higher level administrative jobs to people from all strata of the economy. Such people are charged with the efficient operation of their departments and it is they who provide role models for young people as they grow up. Government operations are not private; they are discussed in schools, reported on in lectures, commented on by candidates for office, and evaluated by those who profess to be enlightening the public. When a government agency is well run, it provides an object lesson for budding managers to emulate; when it is not, it represents a drain on the assets of the taxpayer and a negative object lesson for observers.

The state, in addition to the above, is the source of much of the funding for colleges that prepare individuals for general management or train them as managers in a specific functional area of business. Furthermore, the schools provide a channel by which managers of government enterprise and private industry can funnel their knowledge to one another as well as to the student.

The Place of Education

First, education provides knowledge needed in order to cope with general life experiences: it may be considered as preparation for coping with the broad problems presented by growing up, operating within a family, earning one's living, and being a citizen of the state. Second, education is preparation for dealing with the problems to be solved in building a career, from developing a specialty to functioning at the highest level within that specialty. Education makes the individual a productive member of the economic community by equipping him to exercise a unique skill or perform a needed service, whether this be as an operative, an engineer, or a junior manager. It provides the foundation on which the individual builds an increasing capability to win promotions and to move up in responsibility, authority, and power.

The third function of education is to prepare the individual to cope with change. Technology rapidly changes the workplace; new knowledge quickly makes old practices outmoded; rising costs prevent any organization from accepting a status quo in any area of its operations if it is to survive and grow. A key function of educators is to prepare people to accept change—to adapt to it both emotionally and in practical terms so as to remain productive in society.

Education occurs continuously: as an outgrowth of experiences, through self-development, from exposure to the works of others, and through performance of any worthwhile activity. The major formal role in education, however, is assumed by the schools. They are the main designers of coherent educational programs, delivered in a way that is intended to foster maximum benefit for the time and resources expended, and in subject areas that will prove of longest lasting utility to the resulting educated person. Furthermore, by instilling an interest in learning, they are designed to produce the maximum continuous self-education for the rest of an individual's life. Schools are the greatest proponents of the management process, in that their goal is to educate the student in the most efficiently managed way possible. They become the managerial role model (with all the good and bad connotations of that model) for all those who come in contact with them. Eventually they also teach, as part of their curricula, the process of management itself. Schools seek to develop people who can manage their lives and careers well, whether they enter business, the military, or the government.

The Place of the Employer

When he has first left school, the industrial worker is merely a workman-apprentice, foreman-apprentice, engineer-apprentice, or manager-apprentice. Even if he has studied a specialty, his training is still incomplete, for he lacks experience in the industrial milieu, where the human factors and the commercial struggle take forms that cannot easily be conveyed in the isolated environment of a school. Formal education needs some complement, so where the school's role ends, that of the workplace should begin.

The employer should take responsibility for educating his personnel at all levels and should be constantly on the alert for opportunities to do so. Abilities must be found out, effort encouraged, initiation and training made easier, energy and success rewarded. Thus is a good body of personnel built up.

To whatever grade he belongs, an employee so trained from the inside is better able to fulfill his duties than one introduced from outside, with the exception of the outsider who brings in unique skills to introduce change. To be sure, when an employee of known ability is promoted, there is no guarantee against disappointment. But how much more risky is it to engage someone from outside, even when it appears that every precaution has been taken?

For the technical training of employees of all ranks, learning begins by keeping one's eyes and ears open, blending academic training with common sense, and fulfilling all duties efficiently. When it comes to management, the foregoing practices are still relevant, but additional complexities are encountered in learning through the eyes and ears. Much of a manager's output is the result of his own mental processes, decision making, and problem solving, so the trainee cannot begin by simply observing; he must be actively immersed in duties that require him to immediately apply management tools to the problems of the enterprise.

A sign of good management in a firm is the steady, methodical training of employees at all levels. A few years' competent effort in this regard can yield wonderful results. Conversely, it does not take long for misguided management to nullify the value of good personnel, particularly the potential managerial value of those personnel. If a top manager provides an example in introducing his subordinates as much as possible to the general problems of management, and if they, in turn, do the same for their subordinates, and so on down the hierarchy, skills will be developed in a way that can never be accomplished in a more formal training process. There is little doubt the concern will soon enjoy a well-developed core of managerial talent within the body corporate.

Finally, it is the place of the employer to provide the experience that will prevent the employee from becoming obsolete in his skills, from becoming economically unproductive, and from becoming disillusioned with the career unfolding before him. Some employers will claim that it is the reponsibility of the employee to keep up his interest in his work, the rate of his performance, and whatever it takes to prevent his knowledge from becoming technically outmoded. In truth, however, the structure and nature of the work are the prime determinants of how up-to-date an employee stays. If the latest equipment and newest methods are used in the workplace, and if the employer puts constructive pressure on the employee to maintain his skills with regard to these latest developments, then that employee should not become technically obsolete. If the reward and punishment structure in the workplace is such that at least some rewards are tied to higher output, to innovation, and to the greater success of the firm as it results from an employee's efforts, then that employee will be encouraged to maintain those efforts. And, finally, if the employee is treated with respect by superiors and peers, if his professional integrity is maintained, and if working relationships are harmonious and marked by equitable treatment up and down the line, then that employee will take pride in being a member of the firm and will continue to produce well both quantitatively and qualitatively.

THE NECESSITY FOR TEACHING MANAGEMENT

The work of any organization consists of carrying out the essential technical, accounting, financial, security, and other functions to deliver a product or service to the customer at a fair price. Should any one of these functions not be carried out, the business may founder or, at the very least, will be weakened. Therefore, the body corporate of the concern must be equipped with the knowledge and other tools to perform the functions efficiently, competently, and at reasonable costs. It would be a mistake, however, to limit the training of the individuals within the body corporate to the particular functions to which they are assigned. As a firm grows, the talents and abilities required become more managerial than technical. Accordingly, some management education should be a prerequisite not only at the entry point, but for moving up the hierarchy of the firm.

Some people believe that managerial skills can only be acquired through actual business practice. No one can doubt the value of experience gained by an individual involved with a firm as it goes from small to large, who has advanced from a technical specialty to a management position. However, as a firm moves from small to large, it moves from a risk-taker to a risk-reducer position, and in so doing, cuts the opportunities trainees have to try, to fail, and to try again. When the firm starts protecting itself against mistakes, it fosters decision making by rote so that which worked yesterday is repeated today. A small firm generally lives a very risky existence. Many of its decisions are of a "do or die" nature: it either takes risks and moves forward, or it stays still and surely fails. Its managerial staff absorbs (and learns from) many failures during its growth. The large firm, by contrast, has accrued responsibilities to shareholders, creditors, customers, and to a large number of people who have career investments with that firm. Executives can no longer bet the existence of the firm on the major decisions confronting them. Since the price of failures is so high, those who fail do not survive long with that firm. It takes only one or two bad examples to create an atmosphere that permeates the entire rank of the body corporate—all decision making becomes a matter of minimizing risk (and repeating what worked previously even where inappropriate). Everyone will agree that experience is excellent, but under too many circumstances, meaningful experience is deemed too expensive to be permitted.

Management education should be the foundation on which experience is built. Such education allows the individual to avoid many pitfalls that he would encounter if he were proceeding by trial and error, and allows him to develop breadth of knowledge beyond the experiences he can accrue even in many years of work. It also allows the individual to grasp the ramifications of experiences as they relate to principles he has learned. Thus, he brings a well-structured background to bear on the job instead of regarding his experiences as a series of isolated instances, which are too easily forgotten. The theoretical framework that an individual learns through management education permits the orderly classification and integration of knowledge.

Everyone needs some concepts of management: from the home to affairs of state, the need for managerial ability is always apparent, and is most crucial for individuals who occupy high positions in an enterprise. Hence, there should be some generalized teaching of management—rudimentary in the primary schools, somewhat more sophisticated in the post-primary schools, and quite advanced in higher educational institutions. This teaching will no more make good managers out of all its pupils than technical teaching makes excellent technicians out of all its trainees. Yet management training can be very valuable, so the educational services provided should be analogous to those rendered by technical education. Such services are chiefly a matter of helping young people to understand and effectively use the lessons that will later come their way through experience.

Unfortunately, the beginner has neither management theory nor method, and in this respect some managers remain beginners all their lives. Hence, an effort should be made to spread management ideas throughout all ranks of the population. Obviously, schooling has a large part to play in this teaching. In institutions of higher education, professors can incorporate principles for managing one's own affairs into basic courses, principles for managing the affairs of others at work in more advanced courses, and principles for managing an entire enterprise in still more advanced ones. At the primary school level, of course, the management teachings focus on the rudiments that a child must learn in order to conserve his resources and improve his relationships with others. The rest of the educational spectrum can bridge the gap between the rudimentary and the advanced.

Finally, we come to the question of education for the practicing manager. The world is changing at an increasingly rapid rate, the scope of concerns a manager must confront keeps multiplying in complexity, and the competition which must be met is so fierce that no individual can grow solely through experiences alone. Experiences represent the past and can be expensive teachers. They are risky because they are incomplete, suffer from the narrow view of the individual concerned, and are hard to integrate without a theoretical structure. Constant education is necessary in every management-related aspect of work life. The concept of education, as used here, is very broad. It involves the study of great books, in order to tune up the mind and enable it to break out of narrow ruts; it involves intensive courses at major universities that provide guidance in coping with new developments; it involves constant refresher courses for employees at all levels, so that the latest in theory, research, and the experiences of others can be learned in a way that is coherently integrated with basic principles.

The individual who is aware of his growing responsibilities will not allow himself to remain too narrow in focus as his job becomes more managerial and less technical or specialized. Similarly, the individual who moves into management cannot allow himself to become outdated, to make decisions in areas of which he knows nothing, or to be ignorant of the newest developments which could help his firm grow or meet the competition. Thus, education, as a foundation and as a continuing growth mechanism, is a constant challenge to management.

ADVICE TO COLLEGE GRADUATE FUTURE MANAGERS

As you complete your college studies, you may well be happy in the thought that you are going to be a functioning member of the economy at last, and you probably have the legitimate desire to win a respected position by giving your service. The qualities that you will have to call into play are not precisely those which confer top rank at college. Thus, the art of handling people and the manner in which one carries himself, which are not assessed in examinations, have a certain influence on a budding manager's success. Circumstances, too, vary, so there is nothing surprising in the fact that those at the top of their class are not always the ones who do best. You are not ready to take over the management of a business, even a small one. College has not given you sufficient conceptions of management, of commerce, or of ways of dealing with the complexities presented by customers, the government, unions, and so forth—conceptions that are requisite for an effective manager. Even had it given you them, you would still be lacking in what is known as practical experience, which is acquired only by contact with people and things at work—with you bearing the full consequences of your success or failure in making those contacts productive.

Nor are you ready to run a large technical department straightway, whether that department be in accounting, finance, or engineering. No industrial leader would be rash enough to entrust you immediately with negotiating the financing of a major investment, the sinking of a mineshaft, or the running of a mill. First you must learn the trade. So, like most of your predecessors, you will start as an assistant or even lower down in the hierarchy. Mature judgment is not expected of you, nor practical acquaintance with technical processes, nor wide grasp of the thousand and one details related to your job. But you will be expected to bring, along with your diploma, thoughtfulness, logic, an observant mind, and loyalty as you seek to accomplish your tasks. The theoretical knowledge that you possess will permit you to assimilate quickly all details of any kind of work with which you come in contact.

Your future will rest heavily on your technical abilities, but much more on your managerial abilities. Even for a beginner, knowledge of how to command, plan, organize, and control is the indispensable complement of your technical knowledge in a specific function. You will be judged not on what you know but on what you do, and the beginner accomplishes little without other people's assistance. To know how to handle people is a pressing necessity.

Maintain toward each person, whether he is above or below you in the hierarchy, a professional attitude. Make an effort to earn your superior's good will by carrying out your work energetically and well; do not take advantage of any generalized positive feeling he may have toward you by lessening your efforts. Set out to learn about your subordinates' behavior, character, abilities, accomplishments, and even personal interests. Remember that intelligent individuals capable of making substantial contributions to the firm are to be found at every level in the body corporate. Capable leadership results not merely in discipline, but also in loyalty which may, in difficult or pressing circumstances, bring forth tremendous self-sacrifices on the part of the employees. In working relationships refrain from personal criticisms of others, and whatever negative comments you must make should be directed exclusively at the work product itself, voiced in a professional manner, and constructively aimed at achieving a better result. It is permissible to use criticism when it contributes to improvement, but criticism of any other kind is an act of malevolence or amusement at the expense of others. If you find that a remark you made was based on an inexact interpretation of facts or policies, do not hesitate to acknowledge this openly. In general, as you assess things and people around you, try not to be judgmental, and keep a sense of proportion.

Have confidence in yourself without going so far as to be arrogant. While you should not denigrate or ignore the opinions of others, you should know how to defend your own point of view with confidence and enthusiasm, when you know your subject and are sure of the position you are taking. You will have difficulty convincing others if you yourself are unconvinced.

Your professional work will not entirely consume your time; there should be opportunity to explore questions that interest you and that you want to delve into further. Spend some of your spare time investigating them; seek out what others have done in the same areas, and see whether some problem or other remains unsolved. Knowledge does not come solely from the performance of one's daily tasks; it is necessary to develop the methodologies further, learn from books and periodicals, and make every effort to apply what has been learned directly to your work. Be a subscribing member of the main societies dealing with your work, follow their meetings, attend their conferences, and seek office so that you may take an active part in the society. In this way, you will come into contact with the eminent people of your profession. Try, as early as possible, to publish journal articles about experiences and knowledge gained in your daily work and about related subjects. Finally, keep abreast of current affairs. You should be aware of the general trends of thought in each sphere of modern society.

Be bold and enthusiastic, as befits youth, and never give way to discouragement. When one has put one's best into one's work and endured weariness and discomfort to bring it to conclusion, one's pains are rewarded. Be enterprising, even daring; fear of responsibility is an index of weakness. Do not forget that all intelligence, effort, and ability devoted to the success of an enterprise may come to nought; circumstances sometimes exert a great influence on business success and consequently on the success of those at the top. But the role of luck must not be overrated; he who succeeds a first time may merely be lucky, but if his success is repeated, his own personal worth has played a chief role in that success.

As a member of the managerial ranks, you have a duty not merely to yourself but to your country, profession, colleagues, superiors, and the firm that you serve. Your bearing, attitude, remarks, and conduct should show that you are precisely aware of your responsibilities.

Appendix I
Brief Biography of Henri Fayol

Henri Fayol was born in 1841 of a family of the French petite bourgeoisie. At age 15 he went to the Lycée at Lyon, where he spent two years. From there he went to the National School of Mines at St. Étienne; at 17, he was the youngest student in his class. At 19 he graduated as a Mining Engineer. He was appointed engineer to the Commentry group of mining pits of the Commentry-Fourchambault Company in 1860. Fayol remained with that firm throughout his long and distinguished business career. He retired from the position of Managing Director in 1918, but remained a director of the company until his death in December 1925, at the age of 84.

As can be seen from Appendix II, which summarizes the various positions Fayol held and his principal publications, his working life fell into the following four periods.

1) From 1860 to 1872, Fayol was a practicing professional engineer. His intellectual effort was largely focused on problems of mining engineering, notably the question of overcoming the fire hazards of coal mining.

2) From 1872 to 1888, he was given greater responsibility as the Director of a group of pits. His studies turned to the geological problems of the area and the factors that determined the lives of the various pits for which he was responsible. The studies he conducted during these years led to his geological monograph on the Commentry coal strata, embodying his theory of deltas, which appeared in three volumes between 1886 and 1893.

3) From 1888 to 1918, Fayol was Managing Director (Directeur General) of the combine, which under his leadership became Commentry-Fourchambault-Decazeville, popularly known as Comambault. The success with which he carried out his duties is one of the romance stories of French industrial history. When he was appointed its Chief Executive in 1888, Commentry-Fourchambault was rapidly going downhill and was on the verge of bankruptcy. No dividend had been paid since 1885. Its metallurgical works of Fourchambault and Montlucon were deeply in the red; its coal strata at Commentry and Montvicq were nearing exhaustion. From the day Fayol took charge, the tide turned. The only works that had to be closed were Fourchambault. Montlucon was kept in action, the only surviving blast furnace in central France. The works at Imphy rapidly attained a leading position as a producer of special steels. The approaching exhaustion of Commentry was forestalled by the purchase of the Bressac pits in 1891 and the pits and works at Decazeville in 1892. Decazeville was a difficult field and had been the cause of long-term economic losses for its owners. It needed all the skill of the engineers Fayol had trained at

Commentry and all of his own scientific genius and practical sense to wring success from an unpromising situation. But it was done. Comambault went on growing. In 1900 it extended its activities into the Eastern coal field with the purchase of Joudreville. During the 1914–1918 World War, this great combine rendered France inestimable service.

When Fayol retired at the age of 77, the company's financial position was unassailable and its staff was of exceptional quality. The period after Fayol's retirement was an especially important one in the revelation of his ideas on the administration of the large industrial enterprise. His writing turned from the narrow technical sphere to a focus on general administration, and major papers in 1900 and 1908 were delivered before prestigious mining societies. The first appearance of the present work, "Administration, Industrielle et Générale," was in the third issue of 1916 of the *Bulletin of the Société de l'Industrie Minérale*. The monograph was no sudden exposition of administrative theory, but rather the fruit of long study and experience as evidenced by his earlier papers. If it had not been for the outbreak of World War I, this summary of his views on administration would have been delivered two years earlier. The demand for it was immediate and persistent. The Société de l'Industrie Minérale issued a first reprint of 2000 copies. The printing was quickly exhausted and was followed by others. By 1925, 15,000 copies had been printed, and Dunod Freres of Paris republished the monograph in book form. The first edition in English, translated by J.A. Coubrough, of the British Xylonite Company, Ltd., was published in the United Kingdom in 1929. An English translation of Fayol's work did not reach the United States until Sir Isaac Pitman and Sons Ltd. published the 1949 translation by Constance Storrs (B.A., A.M.B.I.M.). The book quickly achieved the status of "management classic."

— 4) Although Fayol had retired at a ripe old age, he continued to be active. From 1918 to 1925 he devoted himself to popularizing his Theory of Administration, the fruit of his 30 years of astounding practical success.

During this period he undertook two main tasks. The first was the foundation of a Centre of Administrative Studies. For several years the Centre held weekly meetings attended by eminent men from the most varied professions—writers, philosophers, engineers, soldiers, bankers, officials, and industrialists. Henri Fayol presided at these meetings. A large and authoritative literature developed from them, which was subsequently given wide circulation in schools of commerce and the military.

The second task was the far more difficult venture of trying to persuade government to pay some attention to principles of administration. Fayol had no illusions as to the vastness of the task, but he believed it was possible. His pen was busy, and several important papers resulted. Among the more important interactions with government was one in which he was invited to undertake a complete investigation of the department of the Posts and Telegraphs—resulting in an article in the *Revue Politique et Parlémentaire* discoursing on "the state's administrative ineptitude." In 1923 Fayol took a leading part in the Second International Congress of Administrative Science, held in Brussels. During the 1924 Assembly at the League of Nations he accepted an invitation to address the International Federation of Universities at Geneva on the importance of the doctrine of administration as a contribution to peace.

A description of Fayol in the last year of his life, *Un Grand Ingenieur—Henri Fayol,* by the Students Association of the National School of Mines of St. Etienne, describes him as "still young—upright, smiling, with a penetrating and direct glance. M. Fayol meets you as a friend. His natural air of authority, his kindness, his youthfulness of spirit, which makes him interested in everything, enabling him to be a past master in the art of being a grandfather (and even a great-grandfather) are both impressive and, at the same time, most attractive." At the time of his death, he was actively engaged in investigating the organization of the French tobacco industry—a government monopoly.

Thus Fayol's life embraced four careers rather than one, and in each of them he was preeminent. As a technical man he achieved national distinction for his work in mining engineering. As a geologist he propounded a completely new theory of the formation of coal-bearing strata and supported it with a detailed study of the Commentry district, almost unique as a piece of geological research. As a scientist turned industrial leader he had phenomenal success in both fields. Finally, as a philosopher of administration and as a statesman, he left a mark on the thinking of people in his own and many other countries, a mark no less lasting than that left by Frederick Winslow Taylor, the father of scientific management.

Appendix II
Outline of the Career and
Principal Writings of Henri Fayol

YEAR		EVENT OR POSITION	AGE	DATE	PUBLICATIONS
MAIN	SUBSIDIARY				
1841		Born.			
1856		Lycée de Lyon.	15		
1858		School of Mines, St. Étienne.	17		
1860		Appointed Engineer of the Commentry pits of the S.A. Commentry Fourchambault.	19		
1866		Manager of the Commentry pits.	25		TECHNICAL PUBLICATIONS ON MINING ENGINEERING
1872		General Manager of the Commentry, Montvicq and Berry group of mines.	31		*Articles in the Bulletin of the Société de l'Industrie Minérale*
				1874	Note on the timbering of the Commentry pits.
				1877	Planning mine galleries.
				1878	Note on the erection, removal, and replacement of timbering.
				1879	Structural changes and spontaneous combustion in coal exposed to air.
				1882	Note on the elimination of night shifts in the working of large seams.
				1885	Notes on subsidence due to mining.
					SCIENTIFIC PUBLICATIONS ON THE GEOLOGY OF COAL MEASURES *Proceedings of the Académie des Sciences*
				1881	Four geological studies of the Commentry coal measure.
					Bulletin of the Société de l'Industrie Minérale
1888		Managing Director of Commentry-Fourchambault. Appointed a Chevalier of the Legion of Honour.	47	1886 to 1893	Five issues containing the full text of a geological study of the Commentry coal field, subsequently published as a book in three volumes.
	1891	Purchase of the Bressac mines.			*Bulletin of the Société géologique de France*
	1892	Absorbed the mines and works of Décazeville.		1888	Summary of the theory of deltas and history of the formation of the Commentry basin.
	1900	Purchase of the mines of Joudreville in the Eastern coalfield.		1900	PUBLICATIONS ON ADMINISTRATION Paper on administration to the Congrès des Mines et de la Metallurgie.
				1908	"Discourse on the general principles of administration," Jubilee Congress of the Société de l'Industrie Minérale.
	1913	Appointed an Officer of the Legion of Honour.		1916	"Administration, industrielle et générale," *Bulletin de la Société de l'Industrie Minérale.*
				1917	"Importance of the administrative function in the conduct of business." Paper to the Société d'Encouragement pour l'Industrie Nationale. "A discourse on higher education." Paper to the Société des Ingénieurs Civils de France.

Year		Event or Position	Age	Date	Publications
Main	Subsidiary				
1918		Retired from the Managing Directorship of "Comambault," but remained a Director.	77	1918	"The reform of the public services." Paper to the Cercle du Commerce et de l'Industrie. "Positive administration in industry." Article in *La Technique moderne*.
	1918	Formation of the Centre of Administrative Studies.		1919	"The industrialization of the state," *Bulletin of the Société de l'Industrie Minérale*.
		M. Carlioz appointed professor at the School of Higher Commercial Studies.		1920	Lectures on administration at the École supérieure de guerre and at the Centre des hautes études militaire. Published privately.
				1921	*Administrative Reform of the Posts and Telegraphs*. Pamphlet. "The State cannot administer—the posts and telegraphs." Article in the *Revue Politique et Parlémentaire*. Reproduced in book form by Dunod, Paris.
				1923	"The theory of administration in the state." Paper to the Second International Congress of Administrative Science.

Appendix III
Note on the Backup Research

Throughout the revision process, decisions had to be made on elements of the original book which had become obsolete or were directly contradicted by later research. There were not too many of these instances, but each presented an opportunity to commit some serious errors so they were not taken lightly. Most of them concerned Fayol's critiques of the French government and the educational process (he thought math should not be taught to engineers).

The work of Dr. Gabriel Kovac, a Psychologist and Assistant Professor of Management at New York Institute of Technology, was invaluable. He provided a great deal of the research material used in making the judgments of what should be left out, what should be changed slightly to concur with modern practice, and what should be supplemented to render Fayol's ideas "whole."

Appendix IV
Note on the Language Structure

The original French edition and the following English edition were written in what can only be termed archaic language. The translation from the first language to the second did not improve matters at all. Therefore, in this revision, a great deal of work on sentence structure and general editing were crucial to make the book readable by modern standards. For this, major credit should go to Susan Eno. A graduate of the University of Kansas, where she majored in psychology, she has had extensive experience editing books in the various subjects encompassed by the five schools of management thought. She was, therefore, able to provide not only extensive reconstruction of the flow of the language, but also ideas and input to the content as well.

Appendix V
Additions to Henri Fayol's Ideas

In this revision no attempt was made to make the book a comprehensive management volume or anything more than the survey of management process and its applications that was probably intended by Henri Fayol. What was done was to add ideas and sentences which would correct the original material in light of today's research and practice.

Below are notes indicating which ideas were added. With the exception of Chapter 1, these amounted, in most cases, to not more than a few sentences. In just a few cases, several paragraphs were added to cover the idea. The notes below indicate just which ideas were added to the original text. From these notes, the reader should readily be able to discern what was not in the original text. When in doubt, the reader may safely assume that the material was in Fayol's text. It may have been reworded into more modern terminology, but the idea was there—this is just one measure of how applicable to modern management Fayol's thoughts remain after more than a half century.

Chapter 1: All of Chapter 1 has been added to the original text.

Chapter 2: Comments on the budget and its use in planning versus management versus control. Statements re quality of earnings and preserving the cash assets of the firm. Statements re security protecting the intellectual assets of the firm and risk management. Comments on the computer and MIS in accounting.

Chapter 3: Comments re the sequence of events leading to the construction of a large metallurgical works illustrating the planning process. (This simplified Fayol's original exposition of the process.) How the firm arrives at a picture of its needs in the future. Comments on the use of a plan as a guide to action when the company becomes the target of a liability suit, competitive challenge, etc. In the section on the ten-year plan, comments on technological change and obsolescence. Re the five-year plan: labeled it the strategic plan of the firm and made several comments on what it should contain to amplify the original thoughts. Yearly subplans: idea of key indicators and ratios. Plan contents (a mining and metallurgy firm) added comments such as those on pollution control and international conditions.

Chapter 4: In the list of 16 duties, some clarifying words in 2 and 3. Some words on use of the organization chart to delineate the structure of authority. The names of different types of charts for showing responsibilities and duties in a firm have been added. Description of a textile plant and how it allows wider supervision and the material on shops where garments are sewn by hand, were added to clarify Fayol's original descriptions. The mention that large corporations can be groupings of subsidiary companies. Comment amplified the manner in which the chief executive deals with the abstract and, as one goes down the hierarchy, action evolves into work on the product itself. Remarks are included to counter the general wisdom that as one rises in the hierarchy, the details of the lower level cannot be dismissed. They are needed to evaluate quality of results. The description of Taylor's work has been amplified somewhat to make his system a bit clearer than it was in the original text. The concept of completed staff work was introduced as a staff duty. The concept of the manager as a role model has been expanded somewhat to clarify what Fayol indicated in only a tangential manner. Idea that in the selection of personnel management must be on guard against a widening of mediocrity in the firm. Idea that a poor manager may hire a poorer subordinate to prevent the latter from posing a threat to his own job.

Chapter 5: Only very minor additions of a few words here and there clarified Fayol's original text.

Chapter 6: Comments have been added on steps to follow in dealing with incompetent workers to avoid wrongful discharge lawsuits and to afford proper consideration to the employee — that is, giving additional training, warnings, etc.

Chapter 7: Idea that from the commercial standpoint, management must check outgoing and incoming materials for quantity, quality, and price—amplifying Fayol's comments on the subject. Idea that financial executives must manage the firm's liquid assets, establish the most advantageous tax structure, and provide the capital for ensuring growth—updates to Fayol's ideas. Other ideas added: Accounting generates crucial liquidity and other ratios. Security assures protection of the firm's mental and physical assets, and risks that remain are ameliorated by duplication, redundancy, and insurance. The inspector's impartiality rests on complete independence of the inspector vis-à-vis the person or thing being inspected. The inspection department should be isolated from the producing parts of the organization. The inspectors should be isolated from the workers being inspected organizationally, professionally, and even socially.

Chapter 8: Under division of work, Fayol's comments on structure following function are illustrated by a family example. Fayol's material here has been supplemented by judicious additions of material extracted from several places throughout the rest of the book (and deletion from those places). Concepts of job enlargement and job enrichment are introduced to directly amplify Fayol's ideas. Under authority and responsibility, management by objectives, responsibility charting, and work incentive programs are mentioned. Comments on ethics were introduced to amplify Fayol's ideas. Mention of goal-orientation as one safeguard against abuse of authority. Under the section on discipline, discussion of how the nature of agreements has changed in the last half century. Other ideas added: Government intervention has reduced executive responsibility for personnel matters. Every step in the discipline process should reflect concern for the rights of the employee, be free of bias, and be documented. Unity of command is threatened by technological change which has separated authority and responsibility for the decision from the knowledge needed to make that decision. Adaptation to dual command occurs in industries where the technology is extremely complex, rapidly changing, and it is possible to separate functional supervision from formal supervision. In the discussion of piece rates, added emphasis is given to the fact that piecework tends to promote quantity at expense of quality. Stock trading firms use bonuses to reward employees. Bonuses are better than raising a salary base level because high performance may not be sustained—this amplifies what Fayol inferred in his original text. Protecting the firm's interests includes coping with low-cost imports, the high costs of capital, the need to meet technological change with research, and the need to keep productive assets at the cutting edge of technology. Profit-sharing plans do not work for long when tied to savings—when all the fat in operations has been squeezed out, the savings from additional changes are small. Few large firms have profit sharing and it is used as a way of deferring wage increases. Career planning, assessing needs for new managers, developing skills, and determining lines of succession are parts of organization development. What Fayol hints at with regard to abuse of written communications is amplified: too many written communications are grounded in fear and insecurity. The memo is used as a shield.

Chapter 9: Ideas added: The person who builds a career with a firm as it grows from small to large must be able to accept an increasing separation between himself and the actual work of the firm. The single-dimensional thinker grows into a multidimensional thinker as a firm grows and his management position increases in scope. With regard to development of the employee: comments were added on how changes in technology require education to teach how to adapt to them.

Index

Irwin Gray

Born in New York City in 1935, Irwin Gray earned his first university degree in electrical engineering. His second was a Master's degree in electromechanical engineering, his third a Master's degree in business (industrial administration), and his last, a Ph.D. from the Columbia University Graduate School of Business in manpower management.

He started his career as an Engineer with an aerospace firm, moved on to a five-year career with Pan American World Airways as an Electrical Maintenance Engineer and Group Supervisor at the firm's New York base, and then graduated into teaching and consulting. Along the way, he invented a home heating system improvement and for four years headed the firm he started, Envort-Gray Corporation. The firm is still active today under Dr. Gray's son and has enlarged its horizons into energy consulting and related fields.

Running Envort-Gray, says Dr. Gray, "gave me business experience on the firing line equivalent to a second Ph.D in management. It was there that I really began to appreciate the Fayol message."

He is presently a Professor of business at the New York Institute of Technology and teaches at its campuses on Long Island and in New York City. He is doing research into creative problem-solving. His consulting work is split along engineering and management lines. In the former, he is engaged, as a Licensed Professional Engineer, in energy management consulting for his son's firm. In the latter, he delivers seminars on the results of his research, with the main topics being creative problem-solving and ways of applying the research knowledge to solve difficult managerial and technical problems. The techniques, he reports, are directly applicable to problems with the body corporate because "people problems," while often the most difficult to solve, are open to creative approaches and yield important payoffs for the imaginative, innovative firm.

Dr. Gray is a member of the IEEE, Beta Gamma Sigma, the business honor society, and Tau Beta Pi, the engineering honor society. He is the author of two books: *The Engineer in Transition to Management* (New York: IEEE Press) and *Product Liability: A Management Response* (Amacom). He is also Editor of the quarterly journal *Engineering Management Review* and Editor of the *Engineering Management Society Newsletter.*

Henri Fayol

Engineer, geologist, administrator, and writer, Henri Fayol excelled at every aspect of his long and distinguished business career. He was born in 1841 of a family of French petite bourgeoisie and at 19 graduated from the National School of Mines as a mining engineer.

He started out in 1860 as an engineer with the Commentry-Fourchambault Company, where he remained throughout his lifetime. As Managing Director, he brought the company out from the verge of bankruptcy to become a leading steel producer and mining operation.

He wrote many technical papers on mining engineering and the geology of coal fields, but he later turned his focus to general administration, publishing *General and Industrial Management* in 1916. Upon his retirement from the position of Managing Director in 1918 (he remained a Director of Commentry until his death in 1925), he continued working, devoting himself full-time to popularizing his "Theory of Administration."

Irwin Gray

is a Professor of business at the New York Institute of Technology. He is also a consultant in both the engineering and management fields. He began his career as an engineer with an aerospace firm, then spent five years with Pan Am as an electrical maintenance engineer and group supervisor, and finally moved on to teaching and consulting. He also started his own firm, Envort-Gray Corporation, which specializes in energy consulting.

He holds an undergraduate degree in electrical engineering, a Master's in electromechanical engineering, a Master's in business, and a Ph.D. in manpower management from the Columbia University Graduate School of Business.

Dr. Gray is the author of the IEEE PRESS book *The Engineer in Transition to Management*. He is a member of the IEEE, Beta Gamma Sigma, and Tau Beta Pi.